Leave Only
Footprints

Indian Migrants in Kenya

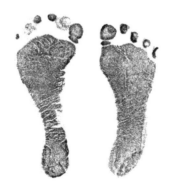

Jaihind S Sumal

Palmetto Publishing Group
Charleston, SC

First Edition

Printed in the United States

ISBN-13: 978-1-64111-295-6
ISBN-10: 1-64111-295-6

Dedicated to our Bebeji Basso
and my parents Kartar Singh and Angrez Kaur Sumal

Not all those who wander are lost.
—TOLKIEN

My grandmother-Bebeji 1942

My parents-Kartar Singh and Angrez Kaur

Table of Contents

Acknowledgments

I am indebted to my father for having the foresight to research and record his experiences both in India and Kenya. He was a self taught man who did not complete his ninth grade schooling but went on to have a good command of written and spoken English, Swahili and a number of Indian languages. He wrote beautiful poetry in both Urdu and Punjabi. His drive for justice and reform got him involved in India's fight for independence and he joined a group of friends to publish a monthly paper in Punjabi. The paper published in Kenya in the 1940s pushed for reforms like simple weddings with no dowries and discouraged outdated Indian traditions and rituals. The facts he recorded for this book in the 1970s and 80s from published material and memory have proved to be accurate when fact checked now. He was a unique father who stimulated our active minds with his engaging stories and discussions. He never pushed his kids to study and taught us to learn not just from books but by engaging in a life of adventure.

I am eternally grateful to my mother who despite having no formal education herself, took a keen interest in our education and encouraged us to work hard and do our best in our studies. She taught us the value of patience and perseverance, the two qualities that have been essential in completing this project.

My siblings were a great help in providing their input to clarify missing information and correcting my interpretation of some events.

I am also thankful to my uncle Gurmukh Singh of San Diego, with whom I was able to spend a day after my father's death, going over Dad's memoirs to look for clarifications, before embarking on this project.

A very special thanks to my younger sister Kamal Dhillon. She worked diligently and spent hours editing, modifying and rearranging the manuscript to make it what it is.

Finally, I would like to thank my nieces Preeti Sumal, Pari Dhillon, my nephew Amar Sumal, my daughter Trishna Patel and my son Aman Sumal for editing and proofreading the book and providing suggestions for improvements.

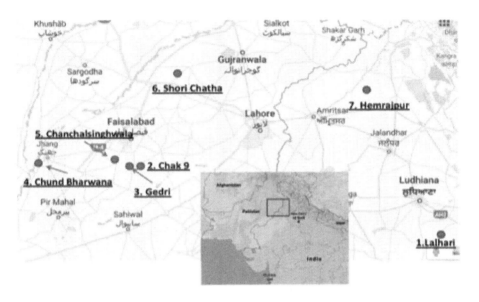

My grandfather, Sham Singh worked as Patwari in seven different locations

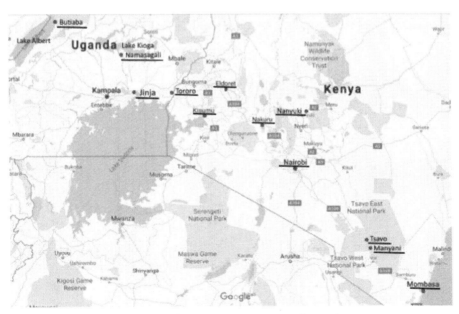

Kartar Singh's footprints in Kenya and Uganda

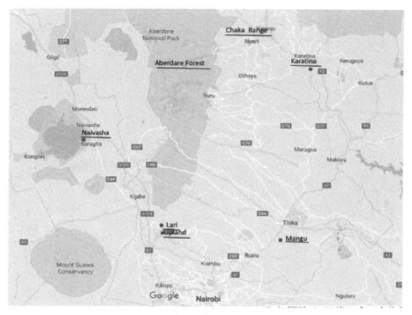

Locations covered in Chapter 7 on Mau Mau

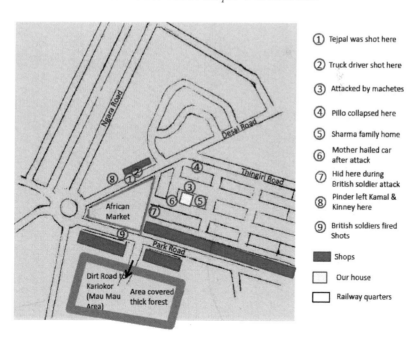

Locations covered in Chapter 7 on Mau Mau - Jaihind's recollections

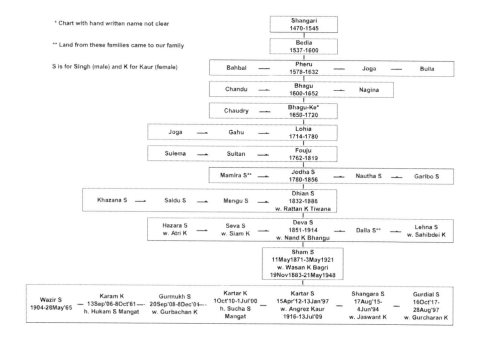

* Chart with hand written name not clear

** Land from these families came to our family

S is for Singh (male) and K for Kaur (female)

Family Tree dating back to 1470

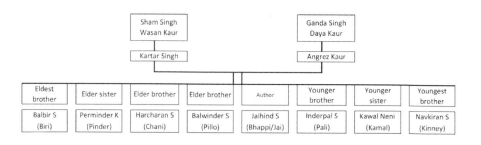

Family Members

Introduction

By Jaihind

This book of my father's and my memoirs, depicts the lives of Indian immigrants in Kenya. Join the journey of my father's early life in India, his migration to British East Africa and our family's life there.

My father, **Kartar Singh Sumal** was a good story teller and as children we would gather on our father's bed and listen to his stories and adventures before falling asleep one by one. We lovingly called our father Chachaji which in Punjabi actually means uncle. His desire to capture his unique life story for the future generations of the family inspired him to record and write his memoirs in the 1970s and 1980s.

To research our ancestral history, my father went to Haridwar, India, where birth and death records have been maintained for centuries by *pundits* (an expert in a particular subject). Ancient records were written on leaves of the birch tree and later transferred to new scrolls. At the time of my father's research, a pundit named Shiv Prasad Vinod Kumar was responsible for our ancestral village in Haridwar and gave my father a copy of the records. The records revealed that over the last five centuries, our ancestors were followers of three of the world's five most populous religions, Hinduism, Islam and Sikhism. My father, although always extremely proud of his Sikh identity, finally emerged as an atheist.

After the early death of my grandfather, my father ran away from home to become a *sadhu* (holy man). His widowed mother's determination to provide a good future for her children saw my father, at a tender age of 15, migrate on his own to British East Africa (Kenya and Uganda), countries that had just opened for large scale migration of Indians seeking better economic futures.

The bulk of migration of Indians from India to Kenya took place between 1910 and 1940. After that immigration was restricted. Most of the migrants were Indians in their teens or twenties, resulting in a population of young immigrant parents and their offspring, with very few grandparents.

My father's life, like most Indians in a racially segregated pre-independence Kenya, was a mixture of suffering indignities at the hands of the white British population, while enjoying the comforts of African domestic servants. The mutual need for family support brought harmony and a distinct identity within the group, independent of religion, caste or language.

Beyond stories of my family, this book will educate you about the political turmoil that resulted from British rule in Kenya, the land that was taken from Africans and the limits that were imposed on their rights. To bring the world's focus to their cause, Africans started to kill and maim both Europeans and Indians. They wanted their land back and be free from the British. This was the start of the Mau Mau Rebellion in Kenya, which is covered here from the perspective of both my father and myself. Europeans called the Mau Mau terrorists, but for Africans they were freedom fighters.

Freedom fighters is how I saw them at the time, and do so to this day. To quash the rebels, Britain sent in its army of men in their late teens or a little older, the majority of whom were British National Servicemen doing their two years compulsory military service. They had little knowledge of Kenya, the locals or their way of life. They were sent to a war at a young age and their arrogance and perhaps their fear made them abuse innocent law-abiding Africans. Us Indians were helplessly caught in the middle and witnessed these atrocities.

Africans took out their frustration and rage on vulnerable Indians, like my brother and I. Our wounded bodies felt the physical pain of the cruel deeds of Africans but our hearts and minds were more scarred by the cruel acts of the British. We were left confused as to who was right and who was wrong. Our parents concentrated on working hard to provide for us and we kept studying hard for a better future. Eventually the comfortable way of life we achieved in Kenya was thrown into disorder by Kenya's independence. The Africanization of Asian jobs and concerns for security led to my father making the big decision to leave Kenya in 1964 to enjoy a retired life in India.

Our fortunes were always closely tied with the British rulers. My grandfather was a Patwari (a local British official), who maintained land ownership records, collected revenue from farmers and controlled the cotton crop in India for export to factories of Britain. The Railways where my father worked transported raw materials, including cotton, from East Africa to ships bound for Britain. Two generations helped to transfer wealth from the colonies on two continents to the British colonial masters.

One by one our family members, like most Kenyan Asians, moved overseas to India, Canada, Britain and the USA leaving behind a wonderful Kenyan life which we will cherish and dream about to our dying days. Moving to the Western countries brought the challenges of having to learn Western ways like using toilet paper and commodes in place of water and squatting, something that cannot be learned from books or classes. We found the people in Britain to be friendly and accommodating, a change from those we had come to know in the colonies. It must have been ironic for my father, during his short stay in UK, to hear cries of "Quit UK" from the far-right conservatives, echoing his cries of "Quit India" from his youth.

On a practical note, I have referred to the people from the Indian subcontinent as 'Indians' for the period before the creation of Pakistan in 1947, and as Asians after that. 'Africans' in the book refers to black indigenous Africans and not Asians and Europeans born in Africa. The United Kingdom is referred to as Britain and its people British. Every name that is in bold letters can be found on the family tree. I have also included maps that help you to visualize the regions where major events took place.

It is my hope that you will find my intimate family history and the unique context in which we were raised to be of an interest to you. In these pages is the story of a family going from riches to poverty in colonial India and a mother's foresight to send her children to a country thousands of miles away. You will learn about the struggles of a family to settle in a new country with its own political internal conflict with their colonial masters. This is a story of Indian migrants in Kenya, which has been captured in personal stories or in its historical aspect in literature of the past, but here it can be seen through the eyes of two generations of our family embarking on this journey.

Our Ancestors

By Kartar

Our Jat Rajput (farmer/warrior) ancestors were part of a large migration from Central India towards West India, to be near the main trade route connecting two big North Indian cities of Lahore and Delhi. Migration was driven mainly by economic opportunities and to a lesser extent, discrimination by Warrior Rajputs against Jat Rajputs. Generations later, similar economic opportunities would take me from this place to the heart of Africa. Our ancestors first moved to a small settlement of farmers and in 1500, **Shangari** (1470-1545; the earliest ancestor who can be tracked down through records) moved to our present-day village Lalheri, near the town of Ludhiana in Punjab state to cultivate one of the semi-arid pieces of land given to farmers.

Hindu priests (Pundits) acted as healers and recommended Hindu prayers and rituals for cures. Sufi Muslim Pirs were an alternative to Pundits as healers. Pirs recommended Muslim prayers and rituals for healing but supported Hindu marriage ceremonies and cremation of dead bodies. By changing healers my ancestors converted from Hinduism to Islam by a simple act of repeating the quote from the Koran required for this conversion. Simple people, simple problems and simple solutions. They became disciples of Sufi Pir Haidar.

The death of the last Mughal Viceroy of Punjab (Adina Beg Khan) in 1758 saw the collapse of Muslim rule in Punjab and the rise of Sikh influence. By 1764 Punjab was split into the Sikh Commonwealth of twelve states (called Misls) under Sikh Chiefs. In our family **Jodha Singh** who died in 1856 was the first to use Singh in his name indicating a conversion from Islam to Sikhism. Once again, the family changed religion not for its ideology but for practical reasons. Like many Punjabis, we became Sikhs partly to associate with the rulers. The conversion to Sikhism did not bring any changes in culture, traditions and ceremonies. Hindu priests continued to conduct most ceremonies and the Indian tradition of caste system was practiced by Hindus, Sikhs and even Muslims. The drive to establish distinct separate cultural norms for Sikhs came later, driven by the Singh Sabha movement.

As in other parts of the world our family changed religion twice to align with the religion of the local rulers, a tradition which was not continued in most of India during the British rule. The British colonists were not like the previous ruling settlers, in that they preferred to look down on the masses and saw themselves as separate to the country they lived in.

CHAPTER I

Riches To Poverty Childhood In Colonial India

By Kartar

My grandfather **Deva Singh** was born in 1851 during the *Sikh Raj* in Punjab, under the leadership of Maharaja Ranjit Singh.

Deva Singh was the eldest of five brothers. After serving in the Sikh army, he ran a small shop in the village and finally settled down as a farmer. He was 27 years old when my grandmother **Nand Kaur** died, leaving behind her only child, my father, who was just seven-year-old at the time. My maternal grandmother came to live in our village to look after my father.

After his wife's death, my grandfather had a number of affairs in the village. He even drew a will leaving all his possessions and land to one of his lady friends. Since the lady could not read, she showed the will to my father, who, without her knowledge removed the section with signatures and seals to make it invalid, thus protecting his rightful inheritance.

I was very scared of my strict grandfather. He looked like a fearsome warrior, with a big turban, curled up mustache and a beard neatly tied in a net. When he died and his body was being prepared for cremation, I walked up to it and stuck my fingers up his nostrils to check if he was still breathing. I had been told that dead people stopped breathing and wanted to make sure he was actually dead. I had done the same a year earlier when he was sleeping, hoping he was dead and was spanked for it.

I called my father, **Sham Singh**, by the name Bhaiyaji. A "ji" at the end of an Indian name is a sign of respect. He was born in 1871, and was an only child.

After finishing high school and passing an examination for agricultural controller in 1891, he got a job as a *patwari*, near our home. A *patwari's* main responsibilities at the time were to collect agricultural revenue for the British, resolve land disputes, and control agricultural production, mainly cotton used in cloth factories of England. This was our family's first service for the colonial masters to support Britain's economy, a service which would span my working life.

My first recollection of my father is of him sitting on a white horse, wearing a white *achkan*, a long coat reaching the knees. He was a man of average height, with a dark complexion. He dressed elegantly and wanted his family to live and dress well and would shower his wife with gold jewelry gifts. He even bought a carriage and horse for his father who sold it and gave the money to his mistress. His job allowed us to live in a large house provided by the government. We enjoyed a good standard of living. My siblings and I felt lucky to have expensive toys to play with, like the wooden rocking horse my father bought for my elder brother.

In large towns like Lyallpur, my father used *tangas* (light horse drawn carriages) to go to work. In small towns, he rode on his own horse. My father was very close to my elder brother and took him along on his visits. I used to cry, sitting in my mother's lap, as I wanted to sit on the horse with my father, but was too young for it.

I wanted to ride his horse so badly, that one day I took it without his permission to the canal half a mile from our house. While crossing a temporary bridge, I slipped off the back of the horse and fell into the running water. Luckily, a canal caretaker, who worked for my father was passing by, and quickly dived in to rescue me.

After seven years of employment, my father was promoted and transferred to Chak 9, a suburb of Faisalabad in Pakistan, about 160 miles away from home. His family decided to find a bride for him before the move. So, at the age of 27, he married my mother, **Wasan Kaur Bagri**, known as Basso by everyone. Her children called her Bebeji.

Bebeji was sixteen at the time, and it was an arranged marriage as most marriages in India were at the time (and many still are). During his career as a *patwari*, my father was posted to six different towns in Northern India and each of his six children, four boys and two girls, were born in a different place. My father was a proud man and stood by his principles, so sometimes would rub his bosses and work colleagues the wrong way. A few of his transfers were for professional development others were due to his differences with his bosses.

I was the fourth of six children and was born at 5 am on Monday April 15, 1912 in a *dak bungalow* (residential building for Government employees) on the banks of a canal of Chenab river, a beautiful rural location in present day Pakistan. The nearest town, Chund Bharwana, was a fair distance away.

A BROTHER FROM A DIFFERENT BACKGROUND

Wazir Singh

An unusual addition to our family was made in Shori Chatha (Pakistan) when I was four years old. A young mother holding her twelve-year-old son by the hand, came to our front door. She had recently lost her husband. She was without any income or family to support her.

"Will you please keep my son?" the woman begged my mother.

"His name is **Wazir**. He can help you around the house. I promise to take him back, as soon as I can support him."

Bebeji hesitated, as she had six children of her own to look after. And then she looked into the little boy's big frightened eyes, and her heart melted. She knew she could not refuse. Wazir settled into our home quietly, always willing to help to show his gratitude. He soon became an integral part of our family.

Life continued smoothly for a year, until my father got transferred to a remote area, unsuitable for raising a family. Bebeji sent a message to Wazir's mother to let her know we were moving back to our ancestral village in Punjab. When she came to take him away, Wazir refused to go with her and never saw her again. Bebeji was touched to hear that Wazir felt so happy and comfortable as part of our family. He always lovingly called her Maa. As he grew up, Wazir stepped in to help his Maa provide for the family, by taking responsibility for the farmland.

He had no friends outside the family and never got married. To find a bride for him in a very conservative society with strict arranged marriage rules and a high ratio of boys to girls would have added to Maa's challenges, so he never mentioned marriage. Wazir always spoke Punjabi with an accent of the Bahawalpur region, which is now in Pakistan. Perhaps, this was his way of staying connected to his roots.

The camel on our farm that we used for drawing irrigation water from the well, became his constant companion. Wazir was happiest spending tranquil days and peaceful nights beside his camel. The farm became his life and the crops thrived under his loving, toiling hands. Perhaps, for the first time in his life, he felt something actually belonged to him. When it got cold, he was known to cover the bulls with his own *razai* (Indian quilt) to ensure they remained fit to work on the farm. Wazir took more care of the land and farm animals than any other family member. He worked on the family farm till his death on May 28, 1965. He was trying to change a wheel on a *gadda* (oxen cart) when it fell on him and he died on the spot. He was 61 years old. After their retirement from Kenya, all of his siblings were in India at the time and he was able to meet them before his death.

At the end of 1917 my father was transferred to Hemrajpur village, his last posting as a *patwari*. He went there on his own. In 1919, after a disagreement with his boss, he resigned and re-joined us in our ancestral village. He started teaching in a local high school at a significantly reduced salary. His income was supplemented by rent from our five and a half acres of agricultural land. Drop in job status and seeing his family suffer due to financial problems led to remorse, depression and heavy drinking.

THE DAY MY FATHER DIED

The trio, my elder brother, younger brother and I used to walk to and from school together. On May 3, 1921, a typical hot summers day, there were just the two of us, my younger brother, **Shangara Singh** and I. My elder brother, **Gurmukh Singh** was at home, looking after my sick father who had been suffering from high fever and stomach pains. The walk back from school in the intense afternoon heat with my brother by my side was slow, interrupted by usual distractions for a seven and nine-year-old.

Our casual, meandering walk turned into quick strides when we saw a group of villagers standing outside our house. We hurried in through our front door when we saw our father lying on the floor in the courtyard, with his head resting on my elder brother Gurmukh Singh's lap. My mother, looking sad, sat quietly beside him. My brother's hand was resting on my father's chest. My father was breathing heavily and tilted his head to look at us as if he had been waiting for us to come home. The look on his face was angelical and peaceful. Soon after, with all of us sitting by his side, he murmured his last words "Ram-Ram" a few times and passed away peacefully at 3 pm.

A *hakim*, a healer using traditional remedies, had been treating my father during his illness. That morning, after we had left for school, the hakim had given him a laxative for his stomach pains, the dose of which was probably too strong for his weakened state. As his condition deteriorated during the day, he was moved to the floor, in keeping with the age-old Indian custom of placing a dying person as close to Mother Earth as possible.

After his last breath, I sat helplessly in stunned silence, my gaze fixed on my father, my ears taking in the noise of people crying around me. Some were sobbing, while others started wailing loudly. The next thing I remember is male family members and close friends moving his body to another side of the courtyard, to be washed and prepared for cremation. My father's body was placed on a funeral pyre in an open field just outside the village, a designated area for cremations. According to tradition, the fire was lit by my elder brother, who was just thirteen at the time. It was a daunting task for a child, but it was seen as a first step in preparing him for his new responsibilities, as head of the family.

I was told that during cremation the soul leaves its earthly form, a concept I struggled to comprehend as a nine-year-old. I had nightmares for a long time after seeing the flames engulf the body that had given me so much love and joy and had always been there whenever I needed it. I often wonder if my endeavor to become a holy man a few years later was a result of my overwhelming desire to search for and connect with the soul that had left my father's body. The truth is that I will never know.

My father left behind a wife and six children. Five of us were still in school. I was nine years old and in the second grade. My eldest sister was still living with us. She had got married a year earlier at the age of fourteen to a boy, **Hukam Singh**, from a nearby village. It was possible to find her an educated husband because of my father's education and social status at the time. In those days a child bride stayed with her family until puberty when *a maclava* (departure) ceremony took place and the bride moved in with her husband's family.

My family's financial situation deteriorated following my father's death. Three years later in 1924, my elder brother Gurmukh Singh left school to supplement our family's income. He went to work as a car driver in Calcutta, but did not like it and returned to the village after a few months. Bebeji took control of finances, something she had never dealt with before. We survived on the income from farm produce, generated by the unconditional devotion of Wazir the gentle, unknown, frightened little boy, who had once entered our home and lives, simply as "The Help."

BEBEJI TAKES THE REINS

Bebeji was from the Jago Hallotali village, which could be reached on foot from our village, an important consideration in selecting a bride in those days. I loved, worshipped and respected my mother, my Bebeji. She was good looking, had a fair complexion and deep-set eyes. She was a gentle person and avoided domineering women. Due to her friendly and generous nature, neighboring ladies often used to gather at our house.

In those days, after a death, a group of ladies from surrounding villages would visit the family to pay their respects. Before entering the village, they would start wailing loudly and shedding crocodile tears. These were organized groups led by professional, fake mourners. My genuine mother was poor at faking her grief and was always sent to the back of the group, a position she was content with.

When our father died, Bebeji at the age of 39, was left on her own to bring up five of us aged from 3 to 14. Our Bebeji faced hardships and struggled in the male dominated world of the 1920s but always ensured that her four sons were educated.

Some village men would taunt her. They would tell her that if she had married them, she would not be in her present predicament. She sold her gold jewelry for the needs of her family but never sold an inch of our ancestral land, which she believed was her sons' inheritance. She kept one gold necklace and used it for her four sons' weddings, by passing the same necklace on to the next bride. When some village ladies teased her about it, she retorted that she would use it for her grandson's bride too. Her mother, our Naniji stayed with us after my father's death.

Bebeji was kind and fair to her daughters-in-law. She never imposed any restrictions on them regarding dress code, and actually aided them in going out without the restrictive and cumbersome *ghagras* (a simple black garment worn over clothes). She used to accompany them to the bus stop, bring back their *ghagras* and then meet them at the bus stop on their return with the *ghagras*, to ensure they arrived in the village properly covered, avoiding criticism from the village ladies.

During one of our family visits to India, my son **Biri** told Bebeji that we were going away by train. She replied that she dreaded the trains going to Bombay as they always took her family away from her, to go to Kenya. Her family would board a train and she would not see them for a number of years.

Towards the end of World War II, Bebeji developed tuberculosis and got very ill and weak. She could not walk. My younger brother Shangara Singh took care of her and carried her on his back to the toilet and the bathroom. My elder brother and I were in Kenya at the time and were preparing to leave for India to be with her when we got the sad news of her demise. She died on May 21, 1948 at the age of 66.

LIFE IN THE VILLAGE

At the beginning of 1918, our family returned to Lalheri from Hemrajpur. I was admitted into a private school located on the grounds of a local cotton ginnery. It was the year the British celebrated their victory over the Germans (known as Armistice Day, November 11, 1918) by distributing victory song leaflets (*tarana-jung*), toy medals (*tagmas*) and Union Jacks, to school students in India. The celebration of Britain's victory and freedom was contrary to Indians' desire for freedom from Britain.

After four years of primary school education, I joined Public Anglo High School in Khanna and started learning English for the first time. The teaching medium in the primary school was Urdu, the official language of North India at the time. In the ninth class, a friend convinced me to leave school and start serving God. *Sadhus* (Hindu religious monks) travelled free on the trains in India so, for a free ride we joined a local sadhu as his trainees. One day we left the village on the midnight train without telling anyone at home. After almost a month of living with sadhus in the Hindu holy city of Haridwar and Narash, I got homesick and came back.

I decided to build a small prayer area dedicated to Hindu deities, in a corner of our courtyard. Every day before going to school, I made a few blocks from mud and left them in the sun to dry. After returning from school I used these bricks to build the walls of the pray area. My evenings were spent praying here. During the construction of this area, I suffered from sunstroke and was hospitalized. I was thrilled to receive a bar of soap on discharge and had my first bath with soap.

At the age of fifteen, I left school without appearing for my ninth-class examination. A few months later I once again ran away to the sadhu camp. This time my uncle knew where to find me so he brought me home after just one night's stay.

These were early signs of a streak in me to seek adventure and live on the fringes of society. My mother, having sensed this and seeing me drifting aimlessly, decided migration to Africa would provide better opportunities and a secure future. I jumped at the idea of this new adventure and my elder brother in Uganda put plans in place to make this happen. My mother bought me my first cotton suit, coat and trousers for my journey. Before that I only owned Indian style clothes (*kurta and pajama*).

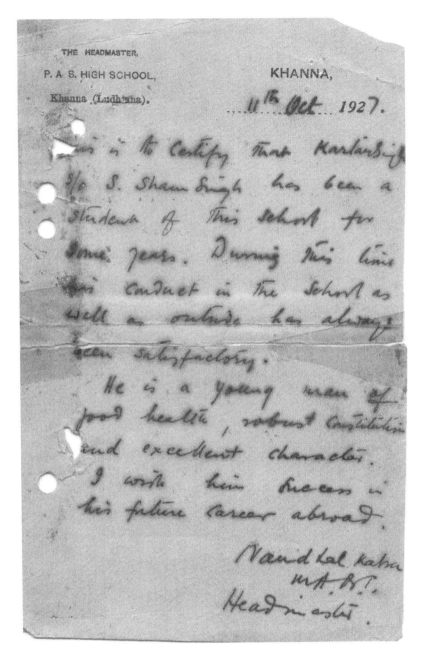

THE HEADMASTER,

P. A. S. HIGH SCHOOL,

Khanna (Ludhiana).

KHANNA,

11th Oct. 1927.

This is to Certify that Kartar Singh s/o S. Sham Singh has been a student of this school for some years. During this time his conduct in the school as well as outside has always been satisfactory.

He is a young man of good health, robust constitution and excellent character. I wish him success in his future career abroad.

Nand Lal Katra
M.A. B.T.
Headmaster.

Kartar's School leaving report

Kartar's school leaving certificate

CHAPTER 2

Kenya, Land Of Promise

By Kartar

In 1920, Chanan Singh Mangat, the first relative in our extended family left for Africa. He had some veterinary experience so he got a job in Kisumu, a port city on Lake Victoria in Kenya and the last station on the recently completed Uganda Railway from Mombasa. Two years later, his younger brother, my elder sister's husband Hukam Singh Mangat joined him. Apart from better job opportunities for new immigrants in small inland towns like Kisumu, the port city had the added attraction of being near Kibos, the only area in Kenya where Indians (mainly Sikhs) were allowed to own farms to grow sugarcane.

In 1925, Chanan Singh came to India on a home visit. My elder sister and brother accompanied him back to Africa. It was common practice for Indians on home visits to take family members and friends with them to settle in the new country which offered better job opportunities with higher earnings. On arrival in Kisumu, my brother Gurmukh Singh worked as a postal clerk. After learning telegraphy, he worked as a postmaster in a number of rural British East African towns. The British wanted to maintain communications between towns, so telegraphy was a desirable administrative skill. At the end of 1927, my brother's friend Rur Singh from Uganda visited us in India. My brother had sent two pocket watches for my younger brother and me. Seeing expensive and not easily available gifts brought back by migrants on leave from African colonies attracted young teenagers to migrate to Africa. A large group of us decided to accompany him on his return to Kenya. There were three from our village, all of different faiths, a Hindu Chaju Ram, a Muslim Rehmat Khan and myself, a Sikh.

Kartar's pocket watch, a gift from elder brother, Gurmukh Singh in 1927

Most of the people in our group were traveling to Kenya for the first time so the visitor showed us how to get our travel documents. From the moment we got our passports, our excitement continued to increase daily, our childlike imagination fueled by stories of the people who had been to Kenya. Listening intently, our active minds could see the adventures and opportunities that would come from this major step in our lives. There was no room for fears of pending dangers. We dreamed of being conquerors and trailblazers. The awe-struck response from their audience encouraged the adventurous story tellers to downplay the negative side.

Parents and families, while supporting us in taking this huge step, had apprehensions about long separations and what it would be like for us to be on our own in an unknown land. My mother and siblings followed the guidance of previous travelers, and helped me pack a few clothes for myself and some for my brother in Kenya in a small suitcase and bedding rolled up and tied with a string. The bedding consisted of a *dhari* (cotton mat), a *razai* (Indian quilt) and a *khesi* (cotton blanket), all made from cotton grown on our farm. She also packed a large tin can of *panjiri* (flour cooked in butter with sugar and nuts added), which was perfect for a long journey, as it was rich in nourishment and stayed edible for weeks even in hot weather. Dry rations like lentils, grains and wheat flour for chapatis, to be cooked on the ship were packed in cloth bags. A few cooking and eating utensils completed the contents of the box.

Soon the big day dawned and a large group from our village and surrounding areas came to bid us farewell at the train station. Long hugs from my mother and siblings ended in watery eyes. The train pulled away and we settled down for our journey to the coast. Based on the experience of those who had taken that journey before us, we had an unwritten guide of where to buy food and stay for the night in Bombay that guaranteed the provider a reliable stream of income and the traveler safety at a fair price.

The long train journey to Bombay was tiring but full of excitement, seeing Indians who dressed differently to us. At the time, Hindi and English were not widely spoken so there was no common language between us and passengers joining or leaving the train. Having left Punjab in the pleasant December weather, the three-day-long train journey ended in the heat and humidity of Bombay. I found the size and dense population of the city overwhelming.

In Bombay, fresh vegetables, fruit, onions (which are an important ingredient for Indian food) and coal for cooking were purchased collectively as a group. Our overnight stay in Bombay was in a cheap hotel where all immigrants from our part of Punjab stayed. We lived nearly a thousand miles from the sea with no lakes nearby, and the largest body of water we had ever seen was a village pond. Nothing compared with our first view of the vast deep blue expanse of the majestic Indian Ocean. We stood staring in awe at the huge ship that was docked, never having seen anything bigger than a mere rowing boat in our lives.

A few of our traveling companions were married. Their wives guided us in collective cooking on the ship. I had never cooked before, and doing it collectively was fun. I picked up a skill that would be handy for my next few years of bachelor life in Kenya. Cooking was done on coal fire stoves in the designated area of the ship. Most meals consisted of lentil curries eaten with chapatis.

After the first few days of excitement on the train and ship, the loneliness of being away from family started creeping in, especially during the silent nights. Lying wrapped up in the warmth and comfort of the cotton bedding from my village reminded me of my carefree days back home. My time away from home as a sadhu had prepared me for a short separation from family but nothing had prepared me for this deep longing to be back within the warmth and love of my family.

We left Bombay on December 16, 1927 on the S.S. Alora. We arrived in Mombasa on 26 December. The S.S. Alora was built in 1882 for transportation of cattle, goods, and passengers between the Mediterranean seaports and UK. The levels above the main deck were for passengers and those below it were for the animals. This ship, along with two others, was later modified to run between the Indian port of Bombay and Kenyan port of Mombasa to ferry Indian passengers. Animal pens were removed to create an open cooking and sleeping area for Indian passengers.

The port city of Mombasa gave us our first glimpse of African police constables who wore a red fez with black tassels, khaki uniforms, but no shoes. Most of the passengers had never seen an African before. With ships arriving from India regularly, the locals were accustomed to the curious stares of the new immigrants. The passengers were transported from ship to land by boats. Immigration and medical checks were done on the ships and customs took place in a building at a boat landing.

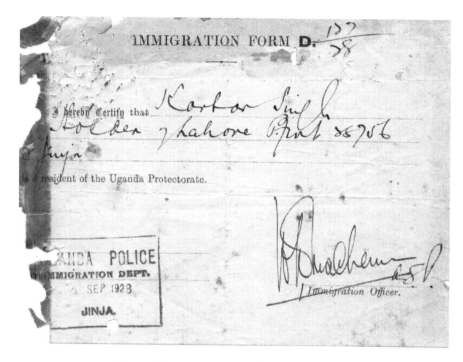

Kartar's Immigration approval (September 1928)

AN UNPLEASANT WELCOME
IN A NEW COUNTRY

We arrived in Mombasa in the morning and left for Nairobi by an evening train. During our short stay in Mombasa we visited a family friend, Tek Singh. We sat down under a mango tree after lunch to play cards, and a few local Indians joined us.

"Can you break a note?" asked a man who was watching the game.

Three of us from the same village, kept our money in one bag that we made the Hindu of our group, who was the oldest of us three, watch over. He gave the man change and we continued playing cards. When we stopped playing, the money bag was gone. To this day I do not know who stole the bag. We reported the theft to police but without any success. I had to borrow money from our host to buy my train ticket.

After traveling in Indian trains, the small passenger coaches of Kenya, lit with kerosene lamps hanging from the roof, seemed like a novelty. The lamp in our coach went out soon after our departure, giving us a beautiful display of the starlit sky as the train snaked its way through the African savannah. Daybreak brought our first glimpse of African wildlife. Everyone pointed out each species that came into view. Some of them we knew from pictures in school books and others were new. Small animals grazed on lush green grass, as giraffes and elephants filled their stomachs on the leaves of acacia trees.

After a night in a Nairobi Hindu temple, we traveled through Rift Valley to the shores of Lake Victoria for an emotional reunion with my elder sister, Karam Kaur in Kisumu. The evening was spent reminiscing about our childhood in India and exchanging news about our family. Just before going to bed, my sister washed my cotton coat and trousers, a parting gift from my mother. They were ready for me to wear the following day to meet my brother.

Early the next morning, we departed on a small ship which took us to Jinja, followed by a short train ride to our destination, Namasagali on the shores of Lake Kioga in Uganda, where my brother was waiting for me. What a joy it was to see him after two years! We gave each other a tight hug. His face revealed the start of a beard, while my baby face only showed a darker shade in the mustache area. We spent the rest of the day in his room, playing catch up.

FINDING GAINFUL EMPLOYMENT

With the British expanding their role in the colonies, it was easy to get employment in the handy trades. My two companions from our village soon got jobs as masons, working for the Railways. Meanwhile I started learning telegraphy from my brother and with a recommendation from the local stationmaster, I got a job in Jinja as a train clerk. I started working on May 17, 1928 at the age of sixteen for 150 Kenyan shillings per month. I put a false date of birth on my application to meet the minimum age requirement of eighteen for employment. No one ever noticed that the age gap between two brothers was just two months, despite being employed in the same department for many years. I became a permanent employee of the Railways seven years later on May 15, 1935.

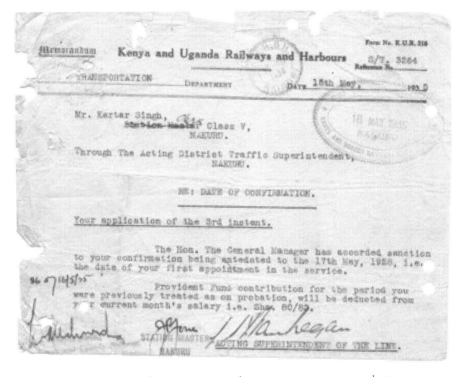

Kartar was made a permanent employee after seven years on probation

In Jinja, which is on the banks of Lake Victoria where the River Nile starts, I shared accommodation with three other bachelors. All of us sent most of our wages to families in India and often ran out of rations in the last week of the month, and lived on boiled potatoes. Each of us would bring our own potato and put it in boiling water on a charcoal stove. As soon as the potatoes were done, we would fight to grab the largest one to quench our hunger. Inder Singh Gill, one of my roommates, who rose to become the first Punjabi millionaire in Kenya, came up with the plan of tying a string to our individual potato, to establish a "potato identity." He also taught us the money saving trick of splitting matchsticks lengthwise to make a box of matches last twice as long. I continued to scrimp and save to send money regularly to the extended family left behind in India.

Migrants lacked immunity and were very susceptible to tropical diseases. Illness, and attacks by wild animals drove a lot of young migrants back to India. People also got homesick, like the two youngsters from my village who returned to India after a few months. I persevered.

A month into the job, I had my first Blackwater fever attack, a form of acute Malaria. Survival rates from the disease at the time were very low. Blackwater fever attacks the kidneys and urine turns blackish with blood, hence the name. I followed the only treatment available, to drink lots of liquids to flush out the system. This helped to get me back on my feet after two months. My brother's visit to see me also greatly boosted my morale.

I had just recovered from my sickness in August 1928 when the then Prince of Wales (later King Edward VIII, who abdicated the British throne to marry American socialite Simpson) was on his way to Makerere University in Uganda and landed by boat in Jinja. The District Commissioner ordered a small number of Railway employees to be present. Apart from me, there were two other Sikhs with turbans in the group. I bowed to the Prince.

"Punjabi hai? (Are you Punjabi?)," he asked me.

"Yes, your Royal Highness" I answered.

"Bohut accha hai (That is good)," he replied.

I felt very proud of that encounter with the future king of Britain.

*(Note from Jaihind: 84 years later my younger brother **Inderpal** received his MBE award from Queen Elizabeth II. Two generations of our family met two monarchs of Britain.)*

Pali receiving his MBE award from Queen Elizabeth II on February 16, 2012

Town officials feared for the Prince's safety when he did not return from a visit to a local African village that evening, but were later relieved to find him having a good time and enjoying a simple meal with an African family.

After seven months in Jinja, I was transferred to Namasagali to work as an assistant pier clerk. My brother and I were thrilled to be reunited. However, disappointment followed soon after as he got transferred to Lugazi. After he left, I shared a small stand-alone room made of wood and tin sheets with a friend.

The completion of the main line from the coast of Kenya to Namasagali brought a weekly passenger train from Nairobi. Most of the passengers on this train were Europeans who would continue their journey from Namasagali by steamer ship SW Grant to ports on Lake Kioga, and from there, further north to Lake Albert with some even going along the Nile River to Egypt. The steamer had cabins for its European passengers. Belgian travelers used the water and land routes to reach Belgian Congo, Uganda's western neighbor. The steamer would leave Namasagali late in the evening and while in port, the Europeans, both local and ship passengers would have their dinner on board, which would be followed by music and dancing on the deck. During my evening walks along the pier I would wonder about their culture, which was very alien to my upbringing in India.

As part of my job, I used to travel on steamer SW Grant from Namasagali to ports on Lake Kioga. For a few months I was transferred to a steamer on the nearby Lake Albert. On one of the trips we stopped at the port of Butiaba. Here the ship's captain was informed about the Lugbara tribe preparing a body for some form of ritual, witchcraft or cannibalism, in a nearby village. The ship captain had the mandate to enforce law and order at ports of call. So, the staff led by the captain, including me and *askaris* (African police constables) went off to investigate.

We reached the location where a body was being prepared amidst some tribal ceremonies. Upon seeing our guns, the locals stopped their activities. The captain asked them to dig a big hole in the ground, place the body in it and pour liquid phenol over them. Phenol was carried on the ship to disinfect bathrooms and toilets. To prevent the locals from digging the body out to eat, they were informed that the liquid was poisonous. Two askaris were left behind to make sure no one disturbed the body.

My second transfer came after a few months stay in Namasagali. Frequent transfers of young Indian railway workers were common. My brother was transferred four times during his six years of service, each time moving closer to the coast, finally ending in Mombasa. With job seniority, the Railways would move staff to larger towns nearer to the coast, while the more remote positions were filled with newcomers from India. Jobs in coastal towns were desirable due to a shorter journey home. After a short stay in Mombasa, my brother resigned from his job and left for India at the end of 1931. At the time I had been in Africa for four years.

Soon after my brother had left for India, one day, just as I was getting ready to play in a local field hockey match, I started feeling ill. This sickness developed into my second attack of Blackwater fever, but this time I was better prepared to deal with my illness. My sister came to look after me and under her loving care, I started recovering slowly. My doctor recommended complete rest and I was granted a medical leave of 100 days to go to India for rehabilitation.

On getting the news of my visit to India, my mother had started looking for, and had successfully found, a bride for me. She was from a nearby village and as was common at the time, the engagement ceremony had been performed in my absence.

While I was in Kenya, on January 2, 1930 my younger sister, **Kartar Kaur**, got married in India. Soon after that my mother started looking for a bride for my elder brother, Gurmukh Singh, who was next in line. Our land was not large and the family was struggling financially after my father's death, an unfavorable status for finding ideal matches. However, my brother's employment in Kenya as a postmaster and his high school education gave him good marriage prospects.

When I was growing up in India, it was common to favor male children. Boys were an asset for farm work and girls were often seen as a burden, due to the dowry needed for their marriage. A lot of villages had a nominated person, normally a woman, who killed girls at birth. The woman in our village who performed this task was Bobi Partapi. This practice resulted in a shortage of females, so boys without any assets like education, a good job, land, or family connections had difficulty finding a bride and would remain bachelors for life.

Working in foreign countries, where wages were usually higher, attracted good marriage proposals. In 1930, my elder brother had a number of proposals. One was from a family in Kenya. Another two were from military families in India, both from girls with high school education. Girls with high school education were rare in those days. However, the proposals fell through when my brother could not get leave to travel to India.

At the end of 1931, my elder brother moved back to India and started a cloth merchant's business in a town near our village. The business was not successful and he soon gave it up. That is when he got his fourth marriage proposal. My elder brother refused it.

"I have no intention of getting married until I have a job and money to support a wife and family," he said.

This is when the family's attention turned to look for a bride for me in earnest.

Kartar before leaving for India to get married

CHAPTER 3

Meeting My Wife

By Kartar

At the age of twenty, I left Kenya for my first visit back home, accompanied by a number of my friends who were all going to India to get married. Like me, some of them were already engaged. Hari Singh, a tailor by trade in the group, agreed to cook for us in return for a share of our rations, which included lentils, wheat flour, eggs, fresh vegetables and live chicken to be slaughtered on the ship. The chickens lived in a ventilated wooden box.

We traveled on S.S. Karagola, which had similar arrangements to S.S. Alora. We got tickets for third class section in open halls below deck where camp beds were available for a small fee. The area had limited ventilation and was very hot so people would move to the cooler deck to sleep in the fresh air, on the covers of the luggage hatches called *falkas*. By the time we boarded the ship most of the *falka* area was occupied.

They say that idle hands are the devil's playground and with all that time on our hands, pranks came naturally to a group of juveniles on a ship.

"Tie me to one of the steel support pillars on the deck with a rope," Hari said and then stuck out his tongue, twisted his hands and feet and made weird noises.

"He is suffering from a rare disease contracted in Africa," I told everyone. "He is going to India for treatment. Be careful, because once in a while, he tends to bite."

Hari then started pulling at the rope, as if he was trying to break loose. Families started to leave the coveted hatch cover area to go below the deck, and we were able to occupy the freed space. The next day the families that had left the area saw Hari playing cards with us, and realized they had been tricked. As I reflected on it later in life, it did not seem fair, but as teenagers it was something we felt proud of.

Hari Singh was a great character and was always joking. However, a day before the ship was due to land at Bombay, he became very quiet and worried that he would have to pay a heavy custom duty on the six yards of thick Chinese silk cloth he had bought in Kenya. The cloth was a gift for his brother's wife who had promised her younger sister's hand in marriage in exchange for the silk. If Hari didn't have enough money for the custom duty, the cloth would be confiscated and it would ruin his chances of getting married.

Losing the roll was like losing a wife, so we came up with a plan. Before the ship docked, we had folded the silk cloth length wise as one does for a turban and placed a piece of short wood in the middle of the knot of hair on his head. We tied the roll of silk onto him like a two feet tall turban that was held in place by the end piece going around his chin, and tied up into a tight knot at the top of the turban.

Bombay's heat, combined with the heavy weight and tightness of the turban made Hari sweat profusely. After the on-board immigration and medical formalities were completed, we exited the ship and entered the Customs Hall. Everyone was staring at Hari. An English customs inspector came over to Hari, walked around him once and then went back to his position. He then asked a junior Sikh customs officer to take off Hari Singh's turban and charge him the appropriate duty.

"Removing a religious symbol from a Sikh's head will have grave consequences," the Sikh officer reminded his English boss. "It could result in local or even national riots."

The customs officer did a search of Hari's suitcase, and found his old turban, a pair of slippers and one or two other trivial items, nothing worth charging a duty on. Once he was outside the Customs Hall, Hari took his turban off and we all celebrated the success of our scheme. As luck would have it, on my return journey to Kenya, Hari and I were on the same ship with our wives.

A three-day train journey brought me back to my village in India after a long four-year absence. A large crowd from my village came to the station to welcome me. My mother and I hugged for a long time.

THE CEREMONY

I got married on April 4, 1932 in India. The night before the wedding, all male members of the wedding party went to the rooftop to sleep. The houses in the village had flat roofs where most people slept during the hot summer nights. I took a duffle bag with me, which I had brought from Kenya. The beds were laid out in rows. They were made of wooden frames with the sleeping surfaces woven from jute strings.

As the groom, I was offered a special bed woven in soft cotton strings, but I didn't need it because I had brought my own. I took out the camping bed from my duffle bag and to the surprise of everyone around me, unfolded it into a full-sized bed. People gathered around it. Some pressed on the cloth surface to see if it could hold a grown person's weight. Others knelt down to see what was underneath it. They had never seen a bed like it before.

The wedding party selected volunteers to take turns to stay awake during the night, to ensure someone would be up at sunrise to wake up the rest of the party.

"I'll take care of it," I said and took out an alarm clock from my bag, wound it up and set the alarm for the appropriate time. The villagers gathered around the clock, another object they had never seen before. They stared at the dial and put their ears next to it to listen to the ticking. The alarm went off the next morning and the wedding party was able to leave on time. A week after the wedding I was lying in my bedroom with the windows wide open. I could hear two women talking outside.

"Have you heard what the magician from Africa did?" one said to another. "The night before the wedding, he took out a handkerchief from his pocket and threw it on the floor and poof! It changed into a bed. Next, he took out a small device from his pocket and twisted its ears. At sunrise the little device pulled up everyone by their shoulders and made them sit up in their beds."

I could not help smiling at the exaggerated version of the power of my modern gadgets in the innocent but overactive imagination of the villagers. Feeling magical, I turned over and fell asleep.

Ours was a Hindu wedding ceremony, as was common in those days. There were about thirty people in the marriage party. My father's cousins were against the marriage, mainly due to jealousy over our success, so they were not invited to the wedding. Since my father was the only son, there were not many people from our side. My mother's brother took my father's place in the ceremonies. The marriage party arrived in *tangas* (two wheeled horse drawn carts), *raths* (covered bullock drawn carts), *gaddas* (uncovered water-buffalo drawn cart), horses and camels.

Someone else in our village was interested in getting married to my wife and started spreading rumors that I was an old man and that my future wife's family were making a big mistake. Before the wedding party reached their village, my bride's uncle came to meet us and requested to see me to make sure I was not an old man.

After the wedding, my mother requested my wife's parents to change her name from Angrez Kaur, an unusual name, to Gurnam Kaur, a more traditional name, but they refused. Angrez means English. I assume the name was chosen to reflect her being statuesque and of fair complexion.

My wife was born in Badochi Kalan, Punjab in 1916. Her birthplace was in the chiefdom of Maharaja of Patiala. Her actual date of birth was never recorded. She was proud of her roots, always emphasizing that Kalan meant a big village. She was the middle one of three sisters. Her only brother, Amar Singh, was the youngest.

My wife never got the education she deserved, as there were no schools for girls in her village. Maharaja Bhupinder Singh of Patiala, although best known for his extravagance and for squandering money on growing his harem, did little for the education of his citizens. My wife was 16 when we got married and I was 20. She possessed a gentle nature and had led a very sheltered life. Before our wedding, her only outings had been to her mother's maternal village or the annual visits to a local temple. Her uncle had served in the British Army, and for a short time was stationed in Kenya during World War I. Some familiarity with Kenya in her family might also have played a role in a marriage that would ultimately take her there.

In July, just over two months after arriving in India, I left for Kenya with my wife by my side. I saw her face for the first time in full daylight on the train journey to Bombay. At the time, it was normal in villages for young brides to cover their faces during the day in the presence of men, including their husbands. The journey from Bombay to Mombasa was rough, due to stormy weather, but we enjoyed the journey in each other's company.

Kartar S 1932   *Angrez K 1937*

Most of the Indian migrants arriving in Kenya in the early 20th century were single men. After finding a job and establishing themselves in the new country, they would return to India to get married. Ships coming back from India would have groups of newly married couples and some brides whose husbands had returned to Kenya on an earlier ship. Brides had to be left behind when men's short leave did not allow enough time to process the paperwork needed for their wives to accompany them back. The unaccompanied brides would travel later with their relatives or friends.

After their weddings in India, two of my friends returned to Kenya alone, waiting for their brides to come on the following ship. It was difficult for them to hide their excitement as the day approached for their brides to arrive. Because brides covered their faces in the presence of their husbands, neither of the friends knew what their wives looked like. Even family friends accompanying the brides had never met the eagerly waiting husbands. On the big day, both friends dressed in their Sunday Best, hurried to the station nearby to bring their wives home.

Later in the morning, I saw one friend walking past our house carrying a suitcase and his wife, with her face covered, followed a few steps behind him. In a similar fashion the second couple went to their house in the opposite direction. I had hardly finished my breakfast when I was informed that the two newly married couples were walking back, towards each other. I was intrigued and rushed out to meet them. I could not hide my amusement when they revealed that after reaching home, to break the ice the two friends had started making small talk with their wives, mainly asking about the health of relatives and friends. The wives had no knowledge of the people they were referring to. That is when they both realized they had gone home with each other's wives and were now walking back to exchange wives for the correct ones!

MY WIFE ADJUSTING TO LIFE IN KENYA

On my return to Kenya, we rented a single room on the first floor of a house near Nairobi train station. Two weeks later my elder sister from Kisumu came to see me and my bride. On her return, my wife accompanied her for a short vacation and to learn more about an Indian wife's role in Kenyan life. It was a big change for her, to be away from the comforts of family life in India, but she adjusted well with support from others.

We later moved to a married quarter, allotted to us by the Railways, and bought two beds, basic crockery, cutlery, and other kitchen utensils. The dishes displayed on the shelves in our living room were a sign of our prosperity and progress. Later, a tea set was added to it. Like most Indians in those days, we had initially used empty tin cans for our daily tea. We bought four used rickety cane chairs, but constantly had to tie their legs with strings to steady them before any guests arrived. With our savings, I also bought my wife a gold set of earrings, necklace, and bangles, and for myself an AJS motorcycle for 150 shillings. One day on my way back from work, I could see my wife and her friends watching me from a distance. To impress them I went fast around a corner and slipped which bruised my body, my bike, and most of all my ego.

My wife missed her family terribly, as we were not able to visit them for another five years. Very few letters were exchanged with her family as her parents were not educated and relied on others to write on their behalf. Her only means of communication with them were those letters, for which she depended on me to read out or reply to. She felt very isolated from her family, but soon built a close-knit network of neighbors and friends. They were all young brides and had also left their families behind in India, so relied on each other for help and support. They taught each other to cook Indian sweets and snacks, to stitch clothes, knit jumpers, embroider sheets and pillowcases, and crochet laces. These tasks were carried out as group activities, while the husbands were at work.

Over the next seven years, I was transferred to three different towns in Kenya for work. Some of those transfers were due to promotion. Each one of my three children was born in different towns: Tororo, Nakuru, and Eldoret. I was following my father's life pattern, with the difference being that I got along well with my bosses. Childhood struggles and my father's impulsive mistake of resigning from his job, had taught me a useful lesson to carefully choose my battles.

A SECOND JOURNEY TO INDIA

On July 12, 1937 at the age of 25, I left Kenya with my family for my second journey home. We were accompanied by my elder brother and my sister's family and we arrived in India in the middle of monsoon season. I soon forgot the tedium of the last part of the journey, where we traveled on oxen carts over muddy roads, upon the excitement of meeting my mother.

My mother had selected a bride for my elder brother, and we were back in India for his wedding. To impress the locals, we dressed in Western attire. My fashionable new shoes, however, were too uncomfortable for our long walk to the bride's village, so I had to carry them in my hands. The groom and I wore suspenders, which added to the villagers' amusement as they assumed that we were wearing our waist belts over our shoulders. After the wedding, our younger brother Shangara Singh and his wife **Jaswant Kaur** also joined us on the journey back to Kenya though his stay there didn't last very long. After four years, both my brothers got homesick and resigned from their jobs to return to India.

Bebeji with her Family Circa 1937
Standing : Gurmukh S, Shangara S, Gurdial S, Kartar S
Sitting Gurbachan K, Kartar K, Bebeji, Karam K, Angrez K
Standing left: Gurmit right: Biri
On floor: Surjit, Baljit and Harpal   In lap: left Pinder and right Baljit S

My wife's father, Ganda Singh died two years later in 1939. He was murdered, due to a mistaken identity, by a distant cousin who had a dispute with his brother over land. My father-in-law was out in the field harvesting sugarcane, when the cousin came from behind and stabbed him, mistaking him for his younger brother.

Traditions and lack of ability to read, write or speak English made it difficult for women to travel alone to and from India. My wife was not able to visit her family at this difficult time. My mother-in-law, **Daya Kaur** died two years later and again my wife was not able to share her grief in person, with her siblings. Her next visit home was in 1942. She was heartbroken to visit the home which she had left five years earlier when both her parents had been alive.

Kartar and Angrez with their 3 eldest children, Biri standing,
Pinder on low stool and Chani on high stool 1941

CHAPTER 4

The Fight For India's Independence

By Kartar

IN KENYA

I took a keen interest in politics and even as a child I always joined village groups in demonstrations against British rule in India. In Kenya I got involved in politics in 1932. The Gadhar party was formed in 1913 by Indians settled in the San Francisco area. It initially published a paper called 'Gadhar ka Gum' which was later renamed to 'Gadhar'. It was an underground paper to support the fight against British rule in India. The paper, published in Urdu and Punjabi, with distribution to overseas Indian communities was banned by the British. A number of Indians in Kenya were involved with this underground paper movement. One of my poems was published under a pen name in the paper on April 13, 1941 (day of Vaisakhi, New Year for Sikhs). The main message of the poem was "For ages you have been slaves to the British rule and have accepted it without a fight, so you have no right to celebrate Vaisakhi". Gadhar Ashram, where the paper was published, was located at 5 Wood Street, San Francisco, California. It is now run by the Indian Consular (Indian Government) and is used for exhibitions.

A local Sikh temple received a regular batch delivery of this paper. A Sikh watchmaker and I were responsible for the distribution of the paper. A competitor Indian Gujarati watchmaker reported our activities to the Railway Headquarters. Learning that, the Railways were preparing orders to sack me. I got really worried and went to see my old boss Lawson, who had been promoted to a senior position in Nairobi. I was able to convince him that in the excitement of my youth I had naively got involved in the paper and was not a revolutionary. I was issued a warning and the case was closed and suspension orders dropped.

IN INDIA

In the early 1940s, there was a lot of political activity in India and I wanted to be part of it. My application for a four month long leave to visit India was approved. On June 17, 1942, at the age of 30, I left Mombasa by ship with my wife and four children to join India's fight for independence. My two politically active friends, Joginder Singh and Bhagat Ram Bhalla, accompanied us. They had resigned from their jobs to go and participate in the movement. Our scheduled stop at Seychelles was prolonged due to a Japanese submarine attack on a ship in the Indian Ocean. We welcomed the delay, because it gave us an opportunity to go sightseeing in an army jeep on the scenic tropical island.

Soon after arriving in India, on August 8, 1942, Mahatma Gandhi made his famous "Quit India" speech and asked for a determined, but passive, resistance, a "Do or Die" call for India's independence from Britain. Gandhi preached nonviolence, but there were also a number of underground parties who wanted to pursue a violent approach. My friend Joginder was already involved with one such group. Given my rebellious streak and desire to serve my homeland, I did not need too much convincing to accompany Joginder to Delhi to join an underground group that was involved in distributing ammunition to Indian extremist groups. We were asked to visit a radio-repair shop in Chandni Chowk area. The shop owner directed us to a doctor and his wife's practice in an area in Old Delhi opposite the railway station, where I was interrogated about my background and intentions.

"I'm not a spy, I'm a freedom fighter," I said and convinced them to let me join the group.

After discussion on a strategy to spread the turmoil in Delhi to the relatively calm cities of Punjab, we were instructed to return to the radio-repair shop. There we were shown a few guns and bullets in the shop's basement. We were told our task was to deliver a package containing two guns and ammunition to a doctor in Ludhiana near my hometown in Punjab.

The plan was for us to catch an evening train from Delhi to Punjab. A package would be delivered to us on the train. Soon after we boarded the train someone brought us a basket full of fruit. We knew the package was under the fruit and I felt very nervous knowing that there was a police superintendent sitting just a few seats away from us. At the next station more police joined to conduct a security check. They did not dig deep into our basket of very ripe fruit, and when they were gone, we took deep sighs of relief.

I hid the basket in a cupboard once we arrived in my village. We split the package between us and delivered the items separately. I got the ammunition and my friend took the guns. I was familiar with Ludhiana, and I agreed to go first. Upon meeting the doctor, I introduced myself and explained the purpose of my visit.

"I've been expecting your arrival," he said.

"Deliver the parcel in person to a village near Raipur, about 30 miles from Ludhiana, to a woman named Mrs. Surjan Singh."

I reached Raipur just as it was getting dark. Mrs. Singh was at home with her seven-year-old son and was hesitant to talk to me until she discovered that we had a mutual friend. Mrs. Singh's sister was married to my friend Ujagar Singh Gill, who worked for the Railways in Kenya. Before leaving Kenya, I had left my belongings at Ujagar's house. She was very concerned about her husband's activities and the danger his family was now in. Surjan Singh was wanted by the police and had gone into hiding. He was later arrested and hanged by the British.

"Give up on this dangerous pursuit and go back to Kenya," Mrs. Singh advised me.

I left for my village, fully convinced to end my gun running activities for the security of my family. However, a month later the patriotic spirit in me was rekindled and I did one more similar run.

During the "Quit India" movement, one of the world's largest civil disobedience protests, the British arrested 60,000 Indians (mostly male political activists), including all the top leaders of the National Congress party. With the male politicians locked up, women started organizing marches and took on some of the political agitation work. The police killed many innocent peaceful demonstrators during protests in major cities of India. On the one-month anniversary of the movement, on September 9, 1942, I participated in a march in Delhi. The march which was led by young girls shouting "Mahatma Gandhi Zindabad, Congress party Zindabad" (*long live Gandhi and Congress party*), ended in four students suffering from gunshot wounds at the hands of the police.

In the evening, I visited my revolutionary friend's house with a renewed sense of defiance and patriotism. A few days later I got a second package to take back to Punjab. This time I delivered the package to Naginder Singh, a freedom fighter in Ludhiana. He was arrested and hanged by the British a year later in 1943. I now shudder to think of my fate if I had got caught, but at the time I was driven by passion to fight for my country's independence.

My family and friends convinced me to stop my gun running activities and go back to Kenya. I had bought tickets for the family to travel on SS Karagola leaving Bombay on October 12, 1942, when my mother requested that I stay in India a little longer. I extended my leave and got a refund on our tickets. And it was a choice that saved our lives, because the ship which we had planned to travel on was sunk in the Indian Ocean by a torpedo fired from a Japanese submarine. I was horrified to hear about the tragic death of my friends from Kenya traveling on that ship.

After this attack, all passenger service between Bombay and East Africa was suspended. My leave expired in October 1942, so my wages stopped too, causing financial hardship for my family. I remained in India until March 1943 when shipping between India and Kenya resumed. I left for Kenya without my family, with just sixteen rupees in my pocket.

In Bombay, I got a pleasant surprise when the Kenyan Government decided to backdate pay for employees stranded in India due to the suspension of shipping services. I sent presents and cash to my family in Punjab, and left Bombay on March 9, 1943 on the boat SS Takliwa and arrived in Mombasa on March 23, 1943.

I lived in a single room in Nairobi, which I shared with my friend Swaran Singh. I left my wife behind in the village, where she took care of our four kids with limited money. Sometimes there was not enough food to go around, but she made sure her kids were fed even if it meant that she would go hungry herself. She didn't complain. My family came to Kenya two years later on June 24, 1945. We carried on living in the single room until the Railways housed us in a better family-oriented area.

This was my last big adventure. After that I strived hard to better the life of my family. My political acts were limited to participating in parades on India's Independence Day. I also became a strong follower of Gandhi and his nonviolent approach, a big change from the earlier violent freedom fighting path taken in my youth.

CHAPTER 5

Life On The Trains Of Kenya

By Kartar

My journey in Kenya started on a train and much of my time there was spent on trains. Kenya, a country the size of France, at the time was sparsely populated with only half a dozen towns. During the long stretches of train journeys through wilderness, I felt fully in control, like a captain on a ship or a pilot on a plane. The train was my domain. The passengers were my children and I had to take care of their various needs. I watched births, deaths, rescues and had wildlife encounters during countless sleepless nights spent on the trains of East African Railways. I also experienced intimidating racist behavior during my employment as Railways goods clerk

FIRE ON THE TRAIN

On a passenger train from Mombasa to Nairobi on May 7, 1956, I looked out of the window and saw smoke coming out of the restaurant car. I quickly pulled the emergency chain. As soon as the train stopped, the English locomotive engineer and I rushed towards the burning restaurant car. The fire was rapidly spreading to the coach next to it.

The scene on the railway line between Emali and Simba yesterday as a first-class coach and a restaurant car of the Mombasa - Nairobi passenger train blazed like torches. Passengers escaped through windows; some were hurt as they fell to the ground. Railway staff were praised for the manner in which they grappled with the burning coaches to separate them from the rest of the train.

Train coaches on fire

It was past midnight, so fortunately the restaurant car was empty, but the first-class coach next to it had passengers sleeping in their berths. We knocked on compartment doors.

"Move through connecting corridors to safer coaches!" we told the passengers.

The High Commissioner for India with his wife and son, the Scottish Caledonian Society Pipe Band returning from a weekend in Mombasa, and a newlywed couple on their honeymoon were in the first-class coach. Passengers scrambled to safety through windows.

I suddenly heard the terrified screams of a mother who believed her daughter was trapped in the burning coach. So, I put on a thick black winter greatcoat issued by the Railways, over my head and ran towards the burning coach. Just as I was stepping in, I heard someone shout that the child had been found safe and sound.

The engineer and I worked out a plan to save the rest of the train. I decoupled the two burning coaches on the caboose side, and signaled the engineer to move the train forward by about a quarter of a mile. I then decoupled the two coaches on the locomotive side and the engineer moved the rest of the train another quarter of a mile, leaving the two blazing coaches isolated in the middle. We cleared a path through the woods along the train track and woke the passengers from the back half of the train, guiding them to the front half. The front half got over-crowded but passengers understood what was going on and were grateful to be rescued.

As we entered Nairobi station, the District Commissioner, the local Press, the station master, the assistant station master and medical personnel were all waiting to welcome us with light refreshments. The passengers who had lost their luggage in the fire were still in their night clothes and the poor honeymoon couple were wrapped in bed sheets. After a day's rest, I returned to work and was informed that my heroic performance in saving lives during the fire had earned me a promotion from a guard to a TTE (*Travelling Ticket Examiner*).

DEATH ON THE TRAIN

Then there was the time that the police constable on the train from Kampala in Uganda to Nairobi in Kenya came to inform me that a passenger was not feeling well. I brought the gentleman and his luggage to my compartment. Soon his face turned pale. His eyes had difficulty focusing and he complained of severe chest pains. I sat next to him as he started talking in a feeble voice.

"I want my luggage and body to be sent back to Uganda," he said.

I tried my best to keep his hopes up but he passed away as soon as the train had crossed into Kenya.

At the next stop I sent a telegram to the next main station, Eldoret, giving details of mileage and time of death. The death had occurred in Kenya, so the body had to be handled by Kenyan authorities. To fulfill the dying man's wishes, the police agreed to my emotional plea of changing the mileage reading to show that the death had occurred while he was still in Uganda. With that his body and luggage was transferred to a train heading in the other direction.

BIRTH ON THE TRAIN

With the train winding through the conical hills near Tsavo National Park, Mrs. Matuko whispered to her husband about her labor pains and sent her anxious husband looking for me, the train ticket examiner. The train *askari* (constable) named Kahindi joined me in preparing an empty compartment into a makeshift delivery room. Mrs. Matuko, followed by an elderly Akamba woman from the same tribe as her, walked into the compartment. And a little while later, there was a tiny passenger without a ticket on the train.

Twins born on train
Kahindi (Askari), Kartar, Mrs. and Mr. Matuko carrying Tabu and Manyani

The father named her Tabu for all the trouble she had caused. *Tabu* in Swahili means trouble. The train chugged along over the flat African savannah with its wealth of animals, including storks. Passing the famous Tsavo River another ticketless passenger arrived on the train. By this time the train had reached Manyani station. With a smile the father said "I am afraid you will have to issue another ticket to this additional passenger. I think we will call her Manyani."

I believe the twins were promised free train travel for life.

ENCOUNTER WITH ANIMALS

Babies weren't the only unexpected guests on the train. One day I was asleep, with my back to the open window, as a herd of elephants walked by. Some of them touched my ears with the tips of their trunks. Each time I thought it was a fly and tried to wave it away with my hands. On about the third time I caught the trunk of one of the elephants. I woke up shocked, started screaming and quickly closed the window.

Then there was the time when our train arrived at Mangu station at 4 am. I saw two animals on the platform and thought they were donkeys, which the Somalis used for carrying goods. I walked down, and saw the station master leaning out of the station building.

"There are lions on the platform!" he shouted.

I was only five to ten feet from what I thought were donkeys until I heard his cries and one of the lion's roar. I dropped the mailbag and quickly ran back into the safety of my coach.

Another time at Voi Station, I was on night duty as an assistant station master when a train coming from Mombasa stopped at the outer signal, and I walked towards the signal box to change it. I saw two eyes shining in the dark and knew it was a lion, so I ran back to the station and closed the door. I found a long bamboo pole and tied my signal lamp to the pole and started waving it from side to side, which meant proceed (up and down meant stop). The driver hesitated for a while but then started to come forward. As the train came into the station, the lion slowly walked away. He was limping a little.

RACIST BOER FROM SOUTH AFRICA

In Eldoret, as a Railway goods clerk, I experienced first-hand the racial prejudice of the Boers (known as *kaburu* by the Africans). They were descendants of the original Dutch settlers of South Africa. In addition to the European and Indian migration to East Africa, there was also a migration of the Boers from South Africa.

In May 1902, the Anglo-Boer War had ended in victory for Britain. The Boers, who did not want to live under British rule, emigrated to other countries, including East Africa. Some came by land and others by sea. Most of them settled around Mount Kilimanjaro in German East Africa. Boers who came by land were experts in driving ox-wagons, a cart pulled by a large team of oxen, which was a useful skill in the early days before the advent of the railroad. After the end of World War I, when Britain took control of Tanganyika (German East Africa) based on the League of Nations mandate, some of the Boers moved to the White Highlands in Kenya mainly around Eldoret area. They left to escape British rule in South Africa and ironically ended up under British rule in Kenya.

I remember a local Boer farmer who rode on horseback, accompanying his truck that carried goods from his farm to the train station. At the loading area, he would sit on his horse, his back upright and straight as a steel rod, taking inventory of his stock. As a goods clerk I had to get his signatures but he would refuse to bend down to me because I was an Indian. I disliked him and his behavior, but had no other option than to stand up on a stool to lift the book up to his level so he could sign it. He behaved in this racist manner towards all Indians and referred to us as coolies, a derogatory term used at the time in South Africa for Indians.

GOODBYE TO EAST AFRICAN RAILWAYS

In early 1962, at the age of 50, I handed in my six months notice of resignation. In my 34 years of service with the Railways, which started as a Goods Clerk, I was promoted to Yard Foreman, Guard, and finally to TTE. These were humble positions, but each promotion was valued and celebrated in my simple life.

The last three positions came with opportunities for overtime and extra money. Most months, I used to work an average of 150 to 200 hours of overtime to provide a comfortable life for my family. I hardly ever took sick leave for fear of losing the overtime income.

Kartar in his Railways' uniform

Kartar with train passengers.
Jaihind, Pali & Kinney standing
in the doorway

CHAPTER 6

Jaihind, Patriotic Name For A Son

By Jaihind

Here is where my story intersects with my father's. My name is **Jaihind**. I was born in the Nagara Maternity Hospital in Nairobi, Kenya in 1946. I was the fifth child, with one sister and three brothers elder to me. At the time of my birth my eldest brother was going through a period of frequent epileptic fits, so to give my mother a break my father decided against home delivery. I was the only child in the family born in a hospital. All other siblings were delivered by midwives at home.

My mother started having contractions late in the evening. There were no taxis or private cars available, so at my father's request, a local coal merchant took my mother to hospital in his delivery truck. I was born early in the morning and given my name Jaihind, which means "Victory to India". My name was inspired by my father's patriotic passion during the struggle for India's independence. Jaihind is also sometimes used as a greeting. It's cited at the end of the Indian national anthem, and for some, it is the name for the Indian flag. Some restaurants and businesses have 'Jaihind' in their name, but I have never met another person who shares my name. Later in life, shaking hands with Indians and saying Jaihind to introduce myself, I would often get the reply "Jaihind" as they mistook my name for a greeting.

Traditionally, Indian women used to cover their heads in the presence of their husbands. After our marriage I used to joke with my wife to cover her head in front of an 'Indian flag'. I would jokingly ask her to say "my son's father" at the end of the Indian national anthem as Indian women were not supposed to utter their husband's name.

My life, despite numerous ups and downs, has been wonderful and joyful on the whole. The downs were made bearable by a wonderful close-knit circle of supportive family and friends. After me, my mother gave birth to two brothers and one sister, each nearly two years apart which made us eight siblings altogether, six brothers and two sisters.

We lived in housing provided by East African Railways, my father's employers. The house had approximately 650 square feet of covered area with one bedroom (17 by 14 feet), one living room (11 feet square) and a small front veranda which was enclosed with wooden sheets. The living room had my father's bed. The enclosed veranda was my elder sister's room and the seven of us together with my mother slept in the big bedroom. There were five beds in the room. A smaller bed in the middle was pushed under one of the bigger beds during the day. My youngest brother slept with my mother and the two eldest brothers had their own beds. The other four of us would share two beds and would swap around. I did not get my own bed until I was in sixth grade.

The Railway housing for Europeans had lighting and power. Asian houses had lighting only, with the exception of a few Asians in senior posts who occupied bigger houses. African houses had no electricity at all. I was about eight years old when I saw my uncle, Shangara Singh, an electrician, install a power outlet in our house for a hot plate, to be used for cooking. I still remember our neighbors coming to see our first green colored hot plate, which was six inches in diameter.

During heavy rains, the wide drain in front of our house used to overflow, completely flooding the small bridge across it. I have a vague memory of nearly drowning in the water. I am told by family members that I fell off the bridge and came out on the other side, waving my arms and legs in the air. Luckily, my father was able to grab my arms and pulled me out just before the water went into the underground drain.

I have painful memories of my childhood, especially ones of my eldest brother having his epileptic fits. My bed was next to a wall with a rough grainy finish. My brother would shake frantically. He was too strong for my mother, who tried to steady him. I would lie awake staring at the wall, afraid to look at my brother. To distract myself, I would stare at the grains, trying to make out different shapes in them. Finally, the commotion would die down and I would once again fall asleep. Us siblings never discussed my brother's condition with each other but listened to our mother talking about it and praying for a cure. At the time there was no treatment for epilepsy.

A RACIALLY SEGREGATED SOCIETY

We lived in a racially segregated society that taught us to see Europeans as a superior race, and we were always striving to reach their economic and social standards. I am not sure if we looked down on Africans, but we certainly took for granted the rather subservient role they performed doing menial tasks to make our lives more comfortable. This was the world we knew and accepted, without challenging it. We were convinced that the color of the skin defined a person. This inferiority complex faded with time, but did not leave our hearts completely.

In restaurants frequented by Europeans, we saw starched white table cloths with cutlery arranged around neatly organized plates and mouth-watering pastries displayed on cake stands, as food was carried to tables by African waiters dressed in starched uniforms. We looked up to these things and dreamed of them, never imagining that we would ever be able to have such privileged lives. In those days, we wouldn't have known how to behave around such luxuries.

In Indian restaurants, the tables usually had Formica tops and food was eaten using our hands or the occasional spoon. Because the three tiers of society never mixed socially, Indians continued to cook their traditional dishes with minimal crossover from other regions of India. The Europeans carried on with their own traditional food while the Africans mainly stuck to their staple diet of Ugali.

We had come to accept our world as being different to that of the whites, and I assume the same was true for the Africans. We never visited a European's house, though my father's English colleague Mr. Good and his family did visit us once for dinner. We never invited or visited an African family in their home.

We endured discrimination against us while ourselves continuing to discriminate against others, just accepting it as the way of life in Kenya.

Residential areas in Kenya's cities were segregated according to race. In Nairobi Indians lived in areas around the middle of the town, with houses built on small plots. Their gardens were either tiny or nonexistent. Europeans lived on the outskirts of the town in big houses with large gardens maintained by their African servants. Africans were confined to shanty areas in a quadrant of the city that stretched from the middle to the outskirts. These areas like Kariokor, Pumwani and Shauri Moyo had limited supplies of water, electricity and sewer services. The buildings were mostly single room cinder block houses or flimsy huts built from tin sheets, wooden pieces and cardboard. African domestic servants for Asian families lived in these areas. There were land deeds in European areas that stated that Asians and Africans could only spend nights in the house as servants. Similarly, Asian areas were restricted for Africans. Only Africans with employment were allowed to live in towns and had to carry an ID Kipande issued by their employers, a cruel and humiliating restriction for the indigenous population living in their own country.

Some of the Indian residential areas in Nairobi were further segregated by religion. There was a Sikh colony and a Goan (Christian) colony. I am not sure of the colonial government's reasoning or motive behind this segregation. When we bought land for our house in a newly opened area in Pangani, the local authority wanted people of the same religion to share a street. There was a street for Sikhs, one for Muslims and so on. Once the Indians became aware of what was going on, they protested and the rule was abolished. Our street initially was just for Sikhs.

It was common for Europeans to have up to four servants: a nanny, a cook, a gardener, and a house servant. Most Asians could only afford a house servant. Where accommodation was available, as in Railway housing, domestic servants would bring their wives and young children to live with them. However most of the African servants had to leave their families behind in their villages. A house servant's duties were usually limited to cleaning the house, washing dishes, making beds, and washing and ironing clothes. In a few houses, their duties included help with cooking and looking after children.

Our servant, Otieno, had a room in the courtyard of our Railway housing. He would help to wash our hands and feet before bedtime. The women of the house did the cooking and grocery shopping. Usually the servants would eat leftovers but occasionally they cooked their own meal of ogali, a mixture of maize and dried bean flour mixed with meat or cooked vegetables, when available. It was common for Asian kids to play with their servant's kids and occasionally eat meals together. However, I never saw an African and Asian kid playing together in the streets. My youngest brother **Kinney** was the same age as our servant's son Ugha and they would spend time playing together and sharing or exchanging food, but only within the four walls of our house.

With Asian parents freed up from household chores, they were able to spend more quality time with their kids, helping them in their education and making them feel more secure. So, in a way, the strong, confident character and success of Asian kids was built on the backs of their Africans servants.

Government jobs in Kenya were also segregated along racial lines, and this extended into most private companies too. Europeans held higher paid jobs mainly as managers. Asians with lower wages were mainly in clerical or supervisory positions, and Africans were relegated to menial tasks with very low compensation. I had never heard of or seen a European working for an Indian or an Indian working for an African. Some jobs, like train conductors and engineers in the Railways were held by both Indians and Europeans. In such cases, the job titles for the races were different. Europeans were "Traveling Ticket Collectors" (TTC) and for exactly the same job, the Asian title was "Traveling Ticket Examiners" (TTE). Wages of a TTC were significantly higher than those of a TTE. The same rule applied to train engine drivers. A European was called a "Train Engineer" and an Asian, just simply, a "Train Driver".

Asian migrants in Kenya endured hardships in new, unfamiliar surroundings in order to educate their children and build confidence in them. They left behind, in India, their baggage of discrimination by religion, caste, social standing, or wealth. The Kenya born generation of Indians and Pakistanis grouped together with their peers to form a very close-knit society and even saw newcomers from the subcontinent as different and looked down upon them.

Amongst Indians, imitating a British accent was seen as a sign of sophistication and people made fun of English spoken with a strong Indian accent.

Indians born in Kenya were multilingual and spoke English, their Indian mother tongue and most could also speak Swahili, albeit with poor grammar, in a dialect called Kitchen Swahili. There were three predominant Indian languages in Kenya, Punjabi, Kutchi (a form of Gujarati) and Konkani. India's national language, Hindi, was spoken within some homes, but never outside, and the same was true for Urdu (a form of Punjabi) which is spoken in Pakistan.

Asians also brought their custom of arranged marriages to East Africa. Selecting one's own partner, termed as 'love marriage' even within the confines of caste and religion was considered scandalous. Europeans and Africans followed their own traditions of choosing a partner. Mixed marriages and relationships were strongly discouraged during colonial rule, perhaps because the British felt that these would undermine their authority. Strong traditions in a close-knit Asian community, which was confined to designated areas, made it difficult for interracial relationships to take root.

In Nairobi, I knew of just four mixed race couples. One was an Indian man who had got married to an English lady he had met while studying in England. I knew three Sikh families with African mothers. European girls seen socializing with Asian boys were either sent back to UK to complete their education or the boy was forced to keep away from the girl by strong arm tactics.

Up until late 1950s, the British kept strict control over the education system as a way to oppress other races in Kenya. There was only one government school for Africans. The only other choice of education available to the Africans was missionary schools, which educated them in ways that kept their loyalties closely aligned with views and religion of their colonial masters. Asian schools had a limited capacity, which was inadequate for the Asian population. There were no primary government schools for Asian girls, so they had to attend private, mostly religious schools. Upon completion of primary school education in seventh grade, there was a state-wide test for Asians to enable only selected students to continue high school education. When I took the test in 1958, only a third of the students qualified for a place in high school. The rest had to go to a trade school or joined their family business. Some were sent to India or Pakistan to complete their education. For Europeans, there was enough capacity for all even up to high school education.

In all Government high schools, blazers, ties, black shoes, and grey shorts, trousers or skirts were mandatory. Adherence to school uniform was strictly checked each morning. Speaking Asian languages in schools was forbidden except in Asian language classes. Breaking this rule resulted in a visit to Principal's office for caning.

Fashions for boys were aligned with those in England. Tight fitting trousers, raised shirt collars, and pointed shoes in the early sixties gave way to bellbottoms, long hair, and tie-dyed clothes during the Beatles era. Girls wore Indian clothes, with their legs always covered, until girls born after 1950 started wearing skirts without *salwaars* (Punjabi trousers). Before the 1950s, Punjabi girls were expected to follow the strict tradition of tying their hair in a single braid until their marriage, after which they could tie it in twin braids or a bun.

The Sikh turban style was also unique. Sikhs from India rolled the muslin cloth, but Sikhs in Kenya folded it into a bandage shape before wrapping it around the head. Kenyan turbans evolved mainly into black or white color and were pointed at the front where as Sikhs in India continued to wear colorful turbans.

ADVENTUROUS SIKHS ON BIKES

During colonial times, most car repair garages and machine shops in Kenya were owned and run by Sikhs. In late 1930s, to prepare for the possibility of WWII hostilities extending to Kenya, 'Indian Manpower Committee' was formed to control Indian artisans in the country. On March 16, 1942 "Defense (Exit Permits) Regulations" were introduced to restrict Indian artisans, mostly machinists and mechanics from leaving the country. This mainly impacted the Sikh community but caused a lot of resentment and anger amongst Indians in general. Isher Dass, a representative for Indians in the Government, was appointed as the Director of 'Indian Manpower Committee', to carry out the dirty work for the colonial Government, of refusing exit visas to Indian artisans trying to visit India, which too was a British colony at the time. Isher Dass's abusive language while callously rejecting visas for urgent family needs made him many enemies in the Indian community. On November 6, 1942, in the presence of his secretary, Dass was assassinated by two Sikhs in his office in Desai Memorial Hall, Nairobi. In a subsequent trial, Balwant Rai and Saran Singh were sentenced to death for murder of Dass and hanged on February 12, 1944. Their bodies were placed in Sikh temples for homage by Indians, followed by a funeral procession through the city to honor them. The procession was attended by more than 10,000 Indians, to send a strong message to the British Government regarding their unjust law.

After the war the Indians continued to hone their trade skills which the next generation of Sikhs born in Kenya, extended into Motorsports. Sikhs were well known for their driving and bike riding skills. Joginder Singh the "Flying Sikh" was the winner of a number of East African and international rallies. "Sagoo brothers" built a single seater racing car from locally available material to race on a Nakuru race track. Sikh champions of local motorbike races inspired me and my close friends Tejpal Bharij and Jagwant Calay to work on a rejected Norton Manx, a complex well known racing bike. We diligently repaired and built the bike to racing standards for Tejpal to competitively participate at the Nakuru race track.

Jaihind on motorbike in Nairobi, Kenya

Adventures involving motorbikes and wildlife came as second nature to Sikhs. The gripping tales of their motorbike adventures were common. The following fictitious narrative during a beer drinking session demonstrates this quality of Sikhs.

This was not your typical Harley Davidson group. Middle aged Sikhs sitting on chairs in a circle with their turbans, long beards and large beer guts looked more like swamis on a hill top. Love of motorcycles was the glue holding the group together. After each sip, the beer glass was placed carefully under their chair. Was it to keep it out of sight of a casual passerby or to hide their sins from God? Stories of motor bike adventures were shared and repeated often. Each repetition slightly different but still held the interest of others.

After a few drinks, and some long winded, detailed discussions about the leg movement of a giraffe, the group was convinced that it would be difficult, but not impossible, to ride a motorbike between the legs of one. The drunken discussions, while debating the physics of a giraffe's anatomy, were peppered with humor, often resulting in hilarious conclusions like "This is nature's way of preventing a bunch of drunken Sikh motorcyclists from riding under the giraffe's belly!"

"It would be the ultimate feat for a motorcyclist!" On that, they all agreed and nodded seriously.

"This could only be accomplished while the animal is running. Only then, does a giraffe swing its hind feet up to plant them far behind the forefeet opening a passage below its belly."

"That is easy! By controlling the speed and the movement of the motorbike between our legs with a twist of the throttle and a gear shift under the foot!" said a drunken Sikh.

They all expressed one unanimous concern, solemnly shaking their heads in unison.

"How could we ever predict the movement of an animal being approached by an unusually fast object and, more importantly, the giraffe's frightened reaction at the sight of a scary Sikh motorbike rider with his head crowned by a turban, the long hair of his beard scattered all over his face and his large belly resting on a fuel tank?"

They all guffawed at this hilarity. Challenges and bets were placed.

Later, my good friend Tejpal Bharij confirmed that his father, Pritam Bharij, with Harbans Dhuperr as his pillion, actually did achieve this feat—not once, but twice. Accomplishment of insurmountable targets makes great legends of people who live lives worth remembering.

CHAPTER 7

The Mau Mau Rebellion

By Kartar and Jaihind

FROM THE PERSPECTIVE OF KARTAR

During colonization of Kenya, European migrants, mainly British moved to the fertile land of white highlands for farming, pushing the Africans to reservations. The first African protests began in the 1920s and were met with hostility and indifference. Tensions continued to rise and during the late 1940s, the Mau Mau movement began, primarily supported by the Kikuyu, Meru, and Embu tribes of the central province of Kenya. These three tribes were closely related, culturally and linguistically. From here on, I will refer to them as the *Kikuyu*. They were a secret group fighting British domination and colonization. Members of the group started taking oaths and they moved their base to the Aberdare Forests and the Mau range.

Working as a Railway Guard had its dangers, during the Mau Mau uprising in Kenya. On March 26, 1953, when the passenger train from Nakuru to Nairobi reached Naivasha station, the stationmaster informed us that we would have to wait for an indefinite period due to a Mau Mau attack on the Lari camp near Upland Station. The Lari Camp mainly housed local Kikuyus, who were loyal to the British Government. It was established to protect occupants from Mau Mau attacks and to cut off supplies to the Mau Mau living in the jungle.

We were also informed that the Mau Mau had raided the police station at Naivasha and stolen guns and ammunition. The raiders had loaded the loot in a truck and were headed towards Lake Naivasha and our passenger train was a possible target for an attack. The station master, who was an African, was instructed to hide all European passengers in the luggage section of the caboose, which had no windows and just one solid door and was impenetrable. The dozen or so European passengers were further protected by armed police guards both inside and outside the door. The Asians and Africans were left defenseless in their coaches.

Looking over the mountains towards Lari, we could see the sky lit up by the burning camp. At around 5am we got the clearance to proceed to Nairobi with a stop at Upland station to collect the injured. On the way, we were stopped at Matipia, a station just before Upland. The station master there told us to remove luggage from the caboose and consolidate third class passengers in order to empty out two third class coaches. It was daylight when we reached Upland, where we were devastated to see injured people and dead bodies strewn across the train platform. In the distance we could still see the huts in Lari camp burning. A bus took some of the injured away to the hospital. We were instructed to load only the injured, and not the dead. We loaded some in the third-class coaches and the rest in the caboose. Upon arriving in Nairobi, the injured were taken to local hospitals in trucks and buses. The famous 'Lari Massacre' and gun haul in Mau Mau hands marked the start of the British recognition of the insurgency as an organized enemy to reckon with.

The spread of the movement happened on the railways, putting staff at risk. I personally had two such dangerous encounters. One was on a cattle train from the foothills of Mount Kenya going from Nanyuki to Nairobi. A steep climb over the Chaka range forced the trains to slow to a crawling pace. The area was controlled by the Mau Mau leader General China. A contingent of the British Security Force was located there to contain and counter the Mau Mau. As our train puffed slowly up the steep hill, two Africans wearing dark clothes climbed onto the caboose. An African attendant accompanying me kicked me lightly, his gaze fixed at the tips of the guns protruding from the intruders' long coats. I understood what was going on. They were members of Mau Mau trying to bypass the British military camp on the train to avoid being caught crossing the area on foot. I asked them to sit down and offered them tea.

After a short silence they asked me, "Are you Pakistan or Nehru?"

"I am Kalasingha and I support Nehru" I replied. (All people of the Sikh religious faith were and are still called Kalasingha in East Africa.)

"Nehru is a good person. He sent lawyers to defend Kenyatta."

I chose not to reply.

It was a short conversation during a very tense 10-mile journey. They jumped off the train after we had passed the camp.

My second encounter with Mau Mau freedom fighters as a Guard on the train was at Makangoo Halt, a lonely spot with nothing else but a watering point for the steam engines before the steep climb towards Mount Kenya. Our train stopped there, and from my seat in the caboose I could hear someone breaking into the train's freight cars (boxcars).

I switched off the light, a normal procedure to prevent the Mau Mau from shooting at us. I looked out of the windows and saw that all of the doors on the two adjoining freight cars were open and around 20 people were unloading sacks of *posho* (beans) off the train. It took the engine 15 minutes to fill up the water tank, while they piled up sacks of posho on both sides of the train. The doors were left hanging open as the train pulled away.

When we reached the next station Karatina, I reported the incident to the stationmaster, who called the local British Military camp. I provided details, but could not tell which direction the raiders took as they were off-loading the freight cars when we left. I went back to the train to complete my report, including an estimated number of bags missing. On my return journey, I was disappointed to learn from the stationmaster that the military had not taken any action for fear of losing their soldiers during a fight in the dark.

FROM THE PERSPECTIVE OF JAIHIND

During the Mau Mau uprising African areas of Nairobi were hot beds for freedom fighters. Our Asian residential area, Nagara, being separated from the African area of Kariokor by just a hundred yards of woodland, was within easy reach of the freedom fighters. Living in Nagara, we were more exposed to Mau Mau activities than those Asians living in areas further away.

On August 8, 1953, we witnessed one of the first casualties in the Asian community. Tejpal, a neighbor one house away left his house to see a movie, with his wife Vidya, 3-year-old daughter Kamlesh, his cousin sister and her husband Kalia. Tejpal worked as a customs officer at Nairobi Airport and had taken a day off work to spend time with his guests. Kalia had come to Nairobi after resigning from his job as the District Commissioner's clerk in Nyeri which, at the time, was the heartland of Mau Mau territory.

Tejpal

Newspaper article on Tejpal's murder

A hundred yards from their house, two African men on a cycle bumped into Tejpal's cousin sister. The family does not know to this day whether it was accidental or deliberate. Her husband Kalia was short tempered and started shouting at the two Africans. One of them pulled out a gun. Kalia ducked. The shot missed him and hit an African driver sitting in the driver seat of a nearby grocery store delivery truck. As Tejpal turned around to see what was happening, the African fired a second shot. The second bullet hit Tejpal. It entered from the left side of his upper torso, went through his lungs and heart and came out on the other side. The bullet was later found in the right sleeve of his jacket.

A group of us were standing outside our house when the family passed us. We ran towards the noise of the gunshots and reached a small group of people standing next to the road. There, we saw Tejpal lying on the ground with his head in his wife's lap. Blood was gushing out from his chest, drenching his wife's sari. She was sobbing and screaming, while people around her tried their best to console her. My eldest brother Biri, and Tejpal's wife's brother, Raj Sharma were in our group and hailed a small delivery truck. Raj, with the help of Biri, laid Tejpal in the truck and drove towards a local hospital. Tejpal passed away en route, leaving behind a shattered family.

After a short time, my elder brother **Pillo**, and I moved away and started walking towards a delivery truck parked next to the shops in a strip mall. Hassan, an African truck driver for Basker Grocery store, always let us climb on the truck's footboard and look at the interior dashboard, a thrill for us kids. My brother rushed to the truck and climbed onto the foot board to look inside and then quickly came down. It was unusual. He would normally take his time to look at everything and talk to the driver. I quickly climbed up to peep inside. The driver was sitting still, holding the steering wheel, with a bullet lodged in his temple. A small amount of blood had trickled down his face and had dried up halfway down his cheek bone. I slowly got down from the footboard and started walking with my brother along the shops. We remained silent, our minds devoid of thoughts and our hearts, numb. The world was empty and frightening. After a short loop along the shops, we arrived home.

Evil acts were taking place outside, but our house felt safe. The stone walls kept evil things from coming in. I never learned any more details about the incident except for rumors that the gun that was used was actually an improvised weapon made from a bicycle frame. The Mau Mau would steal bicycles and use the three tubes from the middle triangular frame of the bicycle as gun barrels. They would put a bullet at one end and use some form of crude improvised mechanism to fire a bullet. There was an article about the incident in the newspapers the following day.

MISTREATMENT OF AFRICANS

In April 1954, the British declared "Operation Anvil" against the Mau Mau, a strong push by the colonial power to defeat the freedom fighters. To strengthen the ranks of whites in Kenya's army, South Africa sent troops to Kenya. Britain started carpet bombing the Aberdare forest, a stronghold of the freedom fighters and pursued collective punishment of the Kikuyu, Meru and Embu tribes.

The British military began conducting random searches in Asian residential areas and went from house to house, pulling out African servants to check their *Kipande ID papers* and Kodi Taxes, a native Hut or Poll tax that Africans purchased; when the value of the stamps reached the tax amount due, they were issued a receipt called Kodi. Africans were taken to an open field and forced to squat in the hot sun for hours in two groups, the ones with valid papers and those without. With the African servants out of the way, the military checked Asian houses, businesses and schools to look for Mau Mau members hiding in there as safe locations.

I remember watching a soldier one day, asking our servant for his papers. When the frightened servant hesitated a little, the soldier slapped him hard in the face. The poor man wet his pants. It was painful to watch a grown up, innocent and kind man being treated like that. This meaningless aggression made me hate white soldiers. At the end of the day, the servants were released, and the Asian employers of those who did not have their ID papers on them had to pay a fine on the spot. The downtrodden Africans felt desperate and frustrated in their own country, and this led them to start attacking innocent civilians like us.

Kipande (ID) for African Servants

ELDEST BROTHER'S DEATH

Biri Circa 1950

The events of October 2, 1954 changed our lives forever. After joining a special police force, which acted as a part time local vigilante group, my father bought a 0.32 bore (caliber) Beretta pistol. This was for his protection during night travel to and from work through Pumwani area, which was the hub of Mau Mau activity in Nairobi. Upon arriving home, he would always make sure the bullets were removed and the gun locked away.

A few days before October 2nd, while coming from work at night, my father saw some Africans running through small lanes towards Pumwani. Further down, policemen looking for the escaped Mau Mau suspects, asked my father if he had seen them. After pointing the police in the right direction, he came home, loaded the pistol and told my mother that he was going back to help the police. My mother got worried when he did not return for a long time.

She did not wake up my eldest brother, as she was afraid he would rush out on his own to look for his father. Also, she was worried that the stressful situation might bring on an epileptic attack. She tried to protect him that night, not knowing what destiny had in store for him. She woke up my elder sister and they both started walking towards my Dad's work. A short distance away they met a policeman who informed them that he had gone with the police and reassured them that they would bring him home safely. Dad returned home very late in the night, totally exhausted and forgot to take the bullets out of the gun.

Since the age of six, Biri, had suffered from epilepsy and had to be withdrawn from school after the third grade due to the severity of his fits. When his health permitted, he had private lessons. With limited qualifications, at the age of seventeen he managed to get a job as a technician with the Railways. A year later, to cover up for a mistake of his own, his crooked boss blamed young and vulnerable Biri for it. Biri's objections were met by harassment from his boss, forcing him to resign. With limited education and health restrictions, Biri had difficulty finding a suitable job. Seeing his friends and relatives progress in their lives, must have been humiliating for him.

A year and a half later, he joined the Railways as a technician but in a different department, so he was happy. As fate would have it, he soon got transferred back to his old department and the harassment resumed. He must have felt trapped and the frequency of his fits increased, due to the stress.

On the evening of October 2, 1954, we excitedly got ready to go to see a Bollywood movie called *Parineeta*. Biri always bought cupcakes as a monthly celebration with the family on payday. It was a boys' night out. My mother, sisters and youngest brother stayed at home.

As we walked back from the movies at 9 pm, Biri, who was 20 at the time, was quiet. I have often wondered, if while watching the movie Biri was reflecting on his own life. Did he relate to the suffering of a character in it or was he thinking of the happy ending that eluded him? We will never know. What we do know is that the recent job transfer had been demoralizing for him. Our parents never discussed it with us and we never brought the subject up, worrying that it would open deep wounds.

My mother had prepared dinner for us when we returned home. The kitchen was in a corner at the far end of the back courtyard and the utensils and groceries were kept in a store on one side of the veranda. My sister **Pinder**, came to fetch utensils from the store and to call us boys for dinner. Biri was standing in the middle of the living room, looking thoughtful and did not say anything. He just nodded. My younger brother **Pali**, aged 6, was sitting there too.

Pinder picked up utensils from the store and had just put them down in the kitchen when we all heard the deafening sound. Everyone rushed to the living room. Biri was lying on the floor and at first, we thought he had had an epileptic fit. It was a gunshot, a shot that pierced our brother's chest and changed our lives forever.

My younger brother Pali, was in the room with Biri when it all happened, and to this day he has difficulty talking or reading about it. I was in the room next door. On hearing the shot, I stood up quickly and saw everyone in the kitchen, led by my father, running towards the living room. I entered the room last.

Biri was on the floor.

"Get some water," asked Mama.

Someone got water in a *garbi*, a metal container. I clearly remember the smell in the room, the smell of residue in the air after a gun fire.

"Go and call Surat Singh," Dad asked my brother Pillo and me.

On the way out, I saw Biri's tied turban still intact, hanging from a hook behind the door. We rushed back home with Dad's friend following us. When we reached home our father was at the front of the house, confused and frantically looking for help. A neighbor, smelling heavily of alcohol was advising our anguished father to wipe fingerprints from the gun using a handkerchief, possibly based on what he had seen in movies. We entered the living room. Some of the neighbors were there. Biri was lying on the floor with his head in Mama's lap. Mama was sobbing loudly. We walked in a daze into the back veranda where the rest of the terrified siblings had gathered. We huddled close to each other, not knowing what to do. Only my elder sister was crying. The rest of us, although terrified, could not fully comprehend the situation and had dry eyes with blank expressions on our faces. After a while our relatives started arriving. A number of the extended family members tried to convince us to eat dinner and tempted us with cakes but none of us showed any interest. We did not enter the living room again.

The next day, in the afternoon, I saw Biri's body on a wooden stretcher in our courtyard, surrounded by women bidding their final farewells before his cremation. I felt sad and knew something terrible had happened, but at the age of eight I did not fully understand what death meant or the impact it would have on those left behind. At the time, my mind was numb with shock and my thoughts were occupied by the events taking place around me. Mama and Pinder were both sitting near Biri's head, stroking his face lovingly and crying. In those days women did not attend cremations. Men were near the backdoor. Biri was carried out through the back door and placed on to a truck. That is the last I saw of him. My elder brothers **Chani** and Pillo went with our Dad to the "Shamshan Bhumi," an open cremation place for Indians, run on donations.

Dad donated 60 shillings on behalf of Biri, whose ashes were immersed in the Indian Ocean, near the Lighthouse at Mombasa. Dad hung a metal plate with a chain around the trunk of a small tree near the Lighthouse which had Biri's name and dates on it. We would visit it on vacation trips to Mombasa. In the summer of 1968 I took my last trip to Mombasa, with my father and the plate was gone.

Biri's death affected us all in different ways. When told that Biri's ashes had been immersed at sea, my younger sister **Kamal** got upset that the fish would hurt him. Dad's hair turned grey almost overnight. My mother would get up at night, and wander towards the kitchen saying that she had to cook food as her children were hungry, or she would go outside saying all the doors were open and she had to shut them. My older sister Pinder would get up, talk to Mama gently, and persuade her to go back to bed.

Witnessing the death of a sibling at a young age scarred us. We clung to each other for comfort. We could not understand how Biri could leave us so suddenly and it took us a long time to realize that it was permanent and he was never going to return to us. Our tragic loss made the bond between us siblings even stronger and it stays so to this day.

For almost a year, neighborhood ladies continued to come to console my mother, but more often it was to discuss their own family problems. I disliked them for making her cry.

In the 1950s in Kenya, people clung to old customs from Punjab's villages. The social codes were very strict. In households that were grieving after a death of a family member, sweet dishes and fried food were frowned upon for a whole year. Sometimes women came during their lunch hour, just to check that we weren't consuming these things. One day one of our younger siblings asked for *poories* (fried flat bread). Mama was scared of the judgmental ladies and was reluctant to make them.

"Mama!" said my elder sister, Pinder, who was seventeen at the time. "Biri's death has shattered our lives! Not the lives of those meddling ladies! They have no right to dictate what we should eat."

"I guess you are right, Pinder."

Mama's love for her children overcame her fear of the judgments of those women and she made some *poories* for us. However, our family chose not to have pastries for a long time, because we associated them with Biri's last moments.

Our father tried to bring a semblance of a normal routine into our lives to help us get over the trauma. He hid his emotions and personal turmoil to present a calm persona to his family. One afternoon when my brother **Chani** walked into the living room, in an otherwise empty house, he found our Dad kneeling on the floor in front of the open trunk containing Biri's belongings, sobbing loudly and uncontrollably. Chani walked away quietly from the heartbreaking image which is still vivid in his mind after 64 years. Six months later, the family had to face another big life changing challenge.

MACHETE ATTACK ON US

It was a nice pleasant evening on April 5, 1955. The setting sun made it difficult to go indoors. After a long walk along a strip of shops, the older boys, including my elder brother Pillo, stood around chatting in a circle. A few feet away, my younger brother Pali, a friend, Pemi Kundi and I sat on a small concrete manhole platform, happily separating the silver parts from the toffee wrappers we had collected. We were only a few yards from our back door.

In the twilight, from the corner of my eye, I saw two men wearing long black coats, enter the street. They looked like upright shadows. There were no street lights and the sunlight was quickly fading. It was difficult to see their faces, though we could make out that they were Africans and as there was nothing unusual about them, we carried on with our task.

As the two men approached us, they suddenly moved towards me, as I was closest to them. One grabbed my arm and hit me on my back. It sounded and felt like he was hitting me with a stick. The "swish"sound was followed by a thud when it hit my body. I cried out and everyone ran away.

The events that transpired after that happened quickly and were difficult to follow. The only thing I clearly remember is that my elder brother, Pillo, turned around to look at me, as the second man moved towards him. I tried to break loose from the grip of the man holding my arm, tearing the short sleeve of my shirt in his hand. His grip slipped and I was able to escape. While running I heard a number of swishing sounds, each followed by a thud, but did not look around to see what was happening.

About twenty yards away, on both sides of the road, there was a gap in the row of houses. I took a right turn. Halfway up the gap I looked around and saw Pillo who had turned left at the gap, running in the opposite direction to me. He was being chased by the two men. This is where I heard the last swish and thud sound.

I took a second right on the road in front of our house and entered the first house, the Sharma family home which had the front door open. Some boys from our group were already there. I could see my younger brother Pali among them.

"The men were attacking us, using sticks!" the older boys told the family.

Nimmo, one of the girls of the Sharma family was staring at my back and suddenly screamed, "There is blood pouring out from your back!"

I didn't feel anything.

"Nimmo, go and get some iodine to clean his wound," said her mother.

It was common for us to use iodine to clean open wounds and I knew how much it hurt when applied. As soon as I heard the word iodine, I ran away through the front door and onto the street.

I started walking towards our house, which was two doors away and I saw my mother walking. She turned around, saw me and rushed to hug me. Her face was tense and expressionless. She moved desperately, as if she was lost. Being with me brought some relief to her.

"Where are your brothers?" she asked.

"**Pali** is safe at our neighbor's house."

"Someone you were with came to the house and told me that your older brother had been attacked by Mau Mau with machetes!"

We started walking towards the direction where Pillo was supposed to be, when my mother saw the blood on my back and I could see the fear in her eyes. She hailed an approaching car. The driver rolled the window down.

"My son has been attacked with machetes. Look at this cut on his back!"

It was the first time I realized that I had been attacked by machetes. Those were not sticks I was beaten with.

According to Indian custom, a married woman would not sit next to a strange man in the front seat of a car. Besides, Mama wanted me to sit close to her, so we both got into the rear seat of the car and the man started driving us to a local hospital. We drove past the place where Pillo was last seen by his friend. There was no one there and the empty street appeared eerie in the darkness of the night. My mother peered frantically through the windows for any signs of my brother, until the driver broke the silence.

"There is no one here so let us take this child to a local hospital for treatment and then start looking for your other son."

I was nine-years-old at the time, Pillo was thirteen and Pali was seven. My uncle had a Ford Prefect and whenever we went to their house for dinner and it got late, he would drop us back at our house in his car. It was something we looked forward to. Most of the time there were up to ten of us in the car, four in the front and six in the back. I always tried to get in the front and positioned my head so I could see the different dials on the dashboard, trying to work out which gauge did what.

Today there were just the three of us in a slightly bigger car. I had a full view of the dashboard but today it was of no interest to me. All I wanted was to see Pillo. The dimly lit side road turned into a well-lit main road. We drove past a building on the right with a big Red Cross sign. A residential building had recently been converted into some form of medical facility.

The bleeding on my back had slowed down significantly, but the wound had started to hurt. I looked at my mother's face. It was tense, but there were no tears.

"Please go a little faster," she pleaded in a calm voice to the driver.

The driver was already trying his best and did not respond.

"I lost my eldest son a few months ago and I cannot lose another one."

"I hear you and I understand," the driver sympathized. "It will be alright this time."

The journey was about fifteen minutes ride before we reached a local hospital, Radiant Health Clinic. Everyone called it Haq's Hospital.

"I am sorry I forgot to wear my headscarf," she said at the end. "I forgot to pick it up in the rush."

We walked quickly to the front desk and my mother asked if my brother had been brought in for treatment. To her disappointment he was not there.

"Please treat my son," she asked the hospital personnel.

Then she asked the man who had given us the lift, to take her to another hospital.

I could feel her pain and did not ask questions or react to her decision to leave me there by myself. I realized later it was the right thing for her to do and I am still amazed that given her circumstances, she made those difficult decisions in such a calm and collected manner.

I was directed to the waiting room and sat on an upright chair. My back and shirt were wet with blood. Every time I leaned back against the chair, my shirt would stick to the wound. When I pulled away from the chair, the cold air would hurt my wound.

News of our attack spread quickly and relatives and friends started coming to the hospital. Someone in a white coat took me into the operating theatre and asked me to lie on my stomach. I was comforted by the presence of my relatives and someone started stitching my wound, without anesthesia or any other medicine. The cut was about eight to ten inches long and I got about 12 stitches. Each time the needle went in, I would faint from the pain and regain consciousness between the stitches. More relatives and friends came into the operating area, trying to find out what happened and who did it. I could only see their faces during the short periods of consciousness but could not answer them.

When it was all done, someone helped me down from the operating table. I saw my uncle, Hukam Singh, who owned the Ford Prefect. He took me to their house. I walked to the car and from the car into their house. I was in a lot of pain due to the stitches. When I reached their house, I was put in a big bed and my aunt, Karam Kaur, my dad's elder sister, cut my shirt with scissors to remove it. I could not move my arms due to the pain. She washed my back with warm water. I do not remember much after that as I must have fallen asleep. This was the first time in my life that I slept in a bed on my own. Us siblings always had to share beds with each other, mostly two to a bed and sometimes three.

The next day I got up, sore and stiff. After breakfast I was anxious to go home to be with my family, especially to see my older brother Pillo. On the way home, we stopped at the hospital to see him. It was a small private hospital which we had passed the previous evening. I got out of the car, eager to see my brother, to show him I was okay.

As soon as I entered the building, the smell reminded me of the previous evening and fear enveloped me. I climbed up the stairs, slowly and cautiously. My brother's room was second on the left. I took each step very carefully, and from the corner of my eye, I saw my brother sitting in his bed. He had tubes sticking out of his nose and bandages on his swollen and somewhat distorted face. I quickly turned around and walked back to the stairs. That image of my brother is still fresh in my mind and I can remember all the details. People around me tried to convince me to go back and meet my brother but nothing could have made me go back. Was it the memory of the previous evening, the face of my brother which looked so different, the tubes around him or the smell of chemicals? I will never know. All I wanted at the time was to get away from that place and go home and see the rest of my family, especially my younger brother Pali.

Over time I learned more about the details of what happened that evening. The two men who attacked us were Mau Mau freedom fighters, wearing long coats to hide their machetes. After being hit on my back, I was able to escape but my brother turned around in response to my cry and it had cost him time. While the others in the group ran away, he was the last in the group and the Mau Mau started attacking him. They struck his upper right arm, trying to cut it off. Next, they hit his neck twice as if to cut his head off. At the gap between the houses where I turned right, he turned left, pursued by his attackers. Halfway up that gap, he must have turned around to see what was going on. That is when they hit his nose with a downward stroke slicing the top layer of his face from the top of the nose to just above his mouth. This was the last swish and thud I heard while running away. After emerging from the gap between the houses they turned left and were in full view of the busy shops. At this spot my brother collapsed in the middle of the road and the attackers ran away, back the way they had come.

Dr. Bhardwaja, a family friend, his brother-in-law Dilbagh and our neighbor Raj were returning from a game of badminton when they heard cries and commotion. The boys running away from the scene informed them that they were being attacked by machetes. They then saw semi-conscious Pillo lying in the middle of the road in a pool of blood. There was blood all over his face with raw exposed flesh in place of the nose. Dr. Bhardwaja first lifted the nose which had flipped down with the machete cut and pressed it against the face and asked Pillo to hold it in place. They then tried to stop the bleeding from his arm by using handkerchiefs as bandages. Dilbagh and Raj hailed a passing car and helped to lay Pillo on the back seat of the car. Dr Bhardwaja accompanied Pillo to a newly opened hospital nearby.

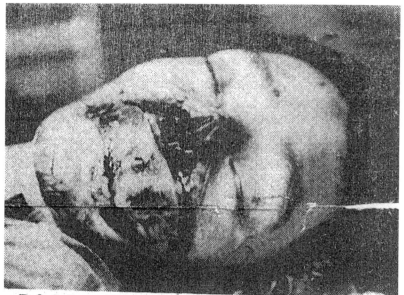

Balwinder with his terribly slashed face as he lay on the operation table for surgeons' skilful needle.

At the hospital, after an initial examination, his condition was deemed as critical with little chance of survival. With other patients needing attention, he was removed from the main operating table and put on an operating theatre cart. One of the new doctors was free and he volunteered to start stitching his face and arm, the two areas of visible cuts on his body, under local anesthesia. The top half of his face was put in place and stitched, followed by stitching on his arm.

Pillo, being a Sikh, had long hair at the time which was covered by a turban. When he collapsed his turban fell off, the knot tying his hair became loose and his hair rolled down to cover his neck and the cuts on it. Since his hair was covered in blood the doctors assumed that the blood was coming from the head. They cut his hair short and that is when they saw the cuts on his neck. They stitched those up next. Since he had lost so much blood someone was sent to get four pints of blood to transfuse. At that time, blood was transferred in glass bottles. On the way back one of the bottles broke in the car but the other three arrived intact and were given to him intravenously.

Pillo was in hospital for about a week. During that time, neither Pali nor I could face visiting him. We got news of his progress from family members. When he came home, I gathered enough courage to meet him. However, it took Pali a few more days to face Pillo.

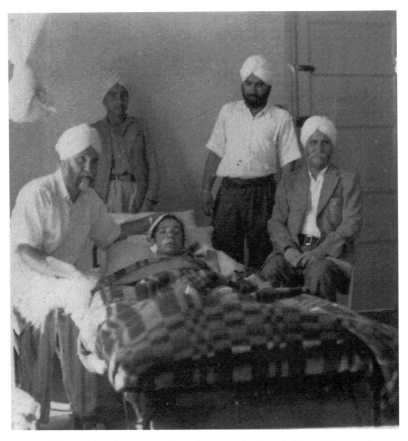

Pillo in hospital recovering from his wounds after the Mau Mau attack

This picture captures well that terrible moment in our lives as Pillo lay in hospital, after the terrifying attack by the Mau Mau. Dad (far left), his face expressing the sadness in his heart, places a comforting and protective hand on Pillo's head. Dad was always very smartly dressed, yet here he is without any concern about his appearance, wearing pyjamas and flip flops. Pillo is lying on a cheap folding bed, bravely holding his head up, with determination in his eyes to beat the odds. On the far right is dad's elder brother Gurmukh Singh with an expressionless sad face. Second from the right is dad's younger brother Shangara Singh concernedly looking at Pillo. Our cousin Sarmukh stands next to the wall with a shocked and scared expression on his young face.

CITY TERRORISTS SLASH ASIAN YOUTHS

On Tuesday evening last, at 7 p.m., some ten or so Asian children were playing in the open space at the back of the Railway Quarters in the Desai Road, Nairobi, when they saw two Africans wearing long coats rambling by. As the Africans were near enough to attack the boys, they suddenly drew pangas and began hitting, two brothers Balwinder Singh (aged 13) and Jaihind Singh (aged 9) receiving the cruel panga blows. Taken by surprise boys scattered promptly and Jaihind Singh succeeded in escaping with a wound in the back. He was not detained at the hospital after the treatment. Balwinder, however was brutally slashed, one blow cutting his nose from under his eyes together with the upper jaw from right, the whole lump sticking out at the left as if on a hinge.

He also received blows across the shoulder over the back and on the arm.

Jaihind Singh (9)   Balwinder Singh (13)

As his good luck would have it the victim was taken charge of in a private nursing home by a band of conscientious doctors under skilled Surgeon B. P. Patel and thanks to Mr. Ahmed Ali's Blood Bank, ample supply of the required blood was readily available. By midnight Balwinder lay on the operation table breathing heavily, all wounds nicely stitched giving everyone hope that he would come through the terrible ordeal. [Photo by Ratan Singh

The attacking Africans were pursued by two K.P.R.s but Asian passers-by lent no assistance in the pursuit—not only that but by their "kya hua," "kyahua" they proved an obstruction, to add to which a passing bus came in between the Terrorists and the pursuers who escaped in the evening's twilight.

Police enquiries continue but no arrests have so far been made. Two points, however, emerge: one is the panga a safe thing in Nairobi—should it not be treated on the same level as a revolver? And secondly, are the Asians careful enough to watch that their boys' quarters are not the meeting places of terrorists? Two recent finds of terrorists' nests with arms stored in them in the middle of the Asian residential areas deserve more serious attention than it has so far received. There are quite a few Asians who do not realise the seriousness of the situation is the conclusion that

"The Nation" article on Mau Mau attack on Balwinder (Pillo) and Jaihind

ASIAN BOYS SLASHED BY AFRICANS

Two boys, one aged 13 and the other nine, the sons of Kartar Singh, Desai Road, Eastleigh, were attacked on Tuesday night while they played outside their home by two Africans armed with pangas.

The elder boy, Balvinder Singh, was taken to Park Road Nursing Home with head injuries. The younger one, Jaihinder Singh, was slashed on the back. He ran to his home to raise the alarm.

After a chase by three members of an Asian Combat Unit who saw the attack, the Africans escaped. Police and General Service Unit patrols scoured the area and an investigation was made by Nairobi City C.I.D.

There were two attacks by Africans on Asians in Nairobi in the early part of February. A man was murdered and a woman and her son were seriously injured.

"East African Standard" article on Mau Mau attack on Balwinder (Pillo) and Jaihind

A few weeks after the incident, a local police detective came to our house to talk to my Dad. After he left, Dad explained to me that the government soldiers had arrested some Mau Mau members and wanted me to identify the two who had attacked us. Days later, he visited us again and this time he was accompanied by another policeman. They both talked to me in my Dad's presence and emphasized the importance of identifying the perpetrators in the line-up so they could be punished for their crimes, thus preventing other children from suffering a similar fate.

FACE TO FACE WITH FREEDOM FIGHTERS

In the evenings, my father used to visit a local Railway Club to join a discussion group on topics of general interest. After the visit of the police detective, a few of my father's friends from this discussion group visited our house and advised me not to point out anyone in the line-up in order to prevent the Mau Mau from taking revenge on our family. This sounded confusing to a nine-year-old boy though I do not recall being distressed by it. Our environment had made us insensitive to it.

A few weeks later the police detective picked me up, along with my father, to take us to the line-up in a railway store yard known as the Goods Shed, a huge enclosed area with materials for railroad tracks and other train repair equipment neatly stacked everywhere. On one of the tracks, there were coaches of a passenger train with window panes that had been replaced by narrowly spaced iron bars. We waited in his car until a group of military personnel came to escort us to the coaches. When we got to the other side of the coaches, we saw about eight members of the Mau Mau standing in a line, looking very frightening and intimidating, some with long braided hair and animal skin covering their bodies. They looked like the pictures of captured Mau Mau members I had seen in newspapers, who after killing an animal would wear the bloody hide and let it dry on their bodies. Since they did not bathe, there was no need to remove the skin from their bodies.

As instructed, I raised my head and faced the line-up, walking like a zombie without any feelings while holding my father's hand. I was asked if I recognized anyone, but I only remembered the two dark shadows walking towards us. I never got a chance to look at them carefully. Even if I had looked at them, it was too dark in the street to see any details. I shook my head to say no.

As we walked back to the car, I held my father's hand tightly. I noticed that the detective had a crooked smoking pipe in his mouth like the one in Sherlock Holmes stories and that he puffed at it when he was nervous. A child's mind shifts attention towards trivial things when faced with something terrifying. On the drive home, like the world around me, the gauges on the car dashboard had no meaning for me.

I heard rumors that General China was in the line-up. He was one of the key leaders of the Mau Mau uprising in Kenya. General China, who was captured a year earlier on January 14, 1954, was never directly linked to any crime. Maybe, I thought, this was an attempt to connect him to our case to prosecute him. In WWII, General China had fought alongside British and American soldiers in Burma where African American soldiers had influenced him to fight the British for independence in his country.

Jaihind and Kartar a few months after the face to face encounter with freedom fighters

COMPENSATION FROM GOVERNMENT

Kenya's government provided funds to cover medical costs and paid compensation to Europeans, Asians, and Africans attacked by the Mau Mau. Hospitals were segregated by races and the level of treatment varied according to race. Apart from medical expenses the compensatory price put on suffering was also based on the color of the skin of the victim.

One year after we were attacked by the Mau Mau on April 5, 1956, Pillo was assessed to have 15% disability and was awarded Kenya Shillings 3600 but my injuries were considered as minor and did not qualify for an award.

With this money and Kenya Shillings 5354 left in my eldest brother Biri's account on his death, my parents bought their first car, an Austin A40 and the rest was put towards a deposit for a house.

Pillo's name and mine were also included in a list of innocent civilian victims of Mau Mau aggression sent by white women settlers in Kenya to the British government asking for their help for better security arrangements for whites in Kenya.

A PETITION FROM THE WOMEN OF KENYA

To   **HER MAJESTY THE QUEEN**

The Humble Petition of the undersigned, Your Majesty's humble and loyal subjects, women of the Colony of Kenya, sheweth as follows :—

1.   That for a considerable time the peace of the Colony of Kenya has been troubled by a savage and cruel gang of rebels known as Mau Mau and that since 1952 a state of emergency has existed in the said Colony.

2.   That on the 24th day of January, 1953, members of Mau Mau murdered Mr. and Mrs. Ruck, the parents of Michael Ruck, a child aged six years, and that thereafter the said members of Mau Mau broke down the door of the room in which Michael Ruck was sleeping and slashed him to death in his bed with pangas.

3.   That on the 26th day of March, 1953, members of Mau Mau murdered many members of the Kikuyu tribe at Lari. According to "The East African Standard" the following events (among many others) took place :—
"In a three and a half hour reign of terror, Mau Mau gangsters massacred between 100 and 150 loyal members of their tribe   They hacked and slashed to pieces men, women and children after firing their homes.
"The small Tigoni hospital was soon crowded out and beds became so scarce that children still covered in congealed blood from their wounds, had to be laid on blankets on the floor.
"One woman in the post said she had been forced to watch while a terrorist held her child and then slowly cut his head in slices as a chef slices an onion.
"Another woman was held by the arms by thugs. She now one of them slit the throat of her young son with a simi and then drink his blood as it gushed out   When this man had finished, he hurled my son's dead body in my face.   Then he slashed me."
"Other wounded reported that they had seen pregnant women slashed across the stomach and then disembowelled in front of their other children.
"One dead baby brought into the police post had not one square inch of skin unbroken on its body."

4.   That on April 3, 1954 Andrew Stephens aged 47 years was hacked and murdered near Nairobi.

5.   That on the 25th day of April, 1953, Mrs. Meloncelli, her daughter Maria, aged 15, and her son, Mario, aged 10, were murdered by Mau Mau.   The terrorists hacked the children to pieces.   From the hacked bodies certain members were torn so that the gang could undertake at once a reiteration of the Mau Mau oath.

6.   That on the 5th day of April, 1955, Balwinder Singh aged 13 years and Jaiwind Singh aged 9 years were hacked and slashed by terrorists in the centre of Nairobi.

7.   That on the 20th day of April, 1955, Geoffrey Danby, aged 15 and Christopher Robin Twohey were hacked or slashed to death by terrorists near Nairobi.

8.   That since the beginning of the emergency many of your Majesty's loyal subjects of all races, men, women and children.

(h)   Though it was known to the authorities or suspected by them that Mau Mau gangsters were in the neighbourhood of the Twohey's house on and before the 20th day of April, 1955, no warning was given to persons in the area, nor were parents advised that children could not safely be allowed to leave the premises of their parents.

10.   That the facts set out above tend to show that even after 2½ years of emergency in the Colony of Kenya, proper steps are not being taken by the Kenya authorities to protect the helpless from Mau Mau terrorists : and that no effective machinery exists in Kenya Colony to ensure that immediate action shall be taken on receipt by the authorities of reports of Mau Mau activities.

Your Majesty's humble and loyal Petitioners therefore respectfully pray :—

(a)   That a Judicial Committee of Enquiry be forthwith despatched from England to the Colony of Kenya with power publicly to enquire into and report on security arrangements for all races.

(b)   That on the report of the said Committee of Enquiry, appropriate instructions be given to the Kenya authorities. AND Your Majesty's humble and loyal Petitioners will ever pray etc.

SIGNATURES		SIGNATURES

Kenyan European women's petition to British government

KILLING OF INNOCENT AFRICANS

By 1955, the British government had intensified their war efforts against the Mau Mau freedom fighters, using ruthless and cruel methods to gain an upper hand. I remember watching detainees from the forests, being brought to Nairobi in trucks which stopped in a playing field near our house, to let them answer the call of nature. I felt consumed with anger, sympathy and helplessness as I witnessed the British soldiers cruelly kicking them as they squatted. We lived in fear of Mau Mau, and helplessly witnessed the cruelty of the British.

With Kenya being on the Equator, we did not experience the four seasons, which makes it difficult for me to pinpoint these incidents to a particular time of the year. This incident I am about to share took place in late 1955 or the first half of 1956. No one I talked to could remember the date. I tried to search in local papers, but did not find anything. With the British controlling the news media, these acts of collective killings were normally not reported in papers.

Because of Nairobi's temperate climate, we were not accustomed to being cooped up indoors. On this day, torrential rain turned into sunshine, which beckoned us to venture outside. Pinder, our elder sister, sensed our eagerness and decided to take the youngest four siblings with her to visit a friend a few hundred yards from our house. On the way, I saw my friend Pemi Kundi, playing in his front yard so I decided to join him. His house was the last one on our street, just before a field used by Africans as an open-air market. Pinder, with my three younger siblings in tow, carried on through the market.

Suddenly, a loud "rat-tat" noise shattered our peaceful surroundings. Someone appeared at the door, from inside the house, shouting for us to come in. We were shocked into stillness for a few moments, which turned into fear as we ran into the house. We heard a few more rounds of that "rat-tat" noise. Someone mentioned a machine gun. We huddled together in a passageway of the house. Our eyes were focused on the front door. We expected the danger outdoors to walk inside at any minute. After a long tense wait, a knock on the door made us all jump with fright. To our surprise and relief, it was Pinder, looking for my younger brother Pali.

She had almost reached the other end of the market when the machine gun firing started. She quickly picked up three-year-old **Kinney**, grabbed five-year-old Kamal's hand, and loudly cried, "Run!" to seven-year-old Pali. As she fled to the other end of the field, she was horrified when she could no longer see Pali. She entered her friend's house and ushered the two little ones towards her friend and then turned around to go back and look for him, but Pinder's friend's mother had locked the front door to prevent anyone from going back into the dangerous market area. Pinder had no time to explain or argue, so she escaped through the back door, frantically looking for her beloved younger brother without a thought for her own life. By then the gun fire had stopped. She knocked on the house where I was and was relieved when she saw Pali with me. He had decided to run back to join me when the gunfire started.

"Stay there," Pinder instructed us both and ran back a third time through the market as she was worried that the two little ones might have followed her out through her friend's back door.

Soon, Pinder returned to take us home. Pali and I followed her out through my friend's front gate. We quietly stared at the ground to avoid looking where gun fire had taken place, and walked slowly away from the market towards the safety of our house until curiosity got the better of me and I turned around to look. Wounded and dead Africans were lying on the ground, with a small number of people tending to them. The rest had fled in fear of their lives.

I recognized the parked green military truck facing us, as a camouflaged, military Bedford truck. The large letters spelling BEDFORD on the front grill confirmed it. Camouflaged, what was it hiding? And from who?

African soldiers placed the bodies of their fellow countrymen in the back of the truck. It was difficult to tell if they were wounded or dead, young or old, male or female. A few British soldiers in starched khaki uniforms with feathered insignias on their berets gave instructions with an outward appearance of softness and order. I wondered if those lying on the ground saw them in the same way. I will never know what happened to the people in the back of that truck. Were there children like us amongst them? What was the impact on their families? How many were left shattered by this? I will never know, though I ask myself these unanswered questions to this day.

We later learned that the British military was chasing a small group of Mau Mau that had escaped from a transporting vehicle when it stopped at the market. The Mau Mau escapees ran into the crowd, which is why the British military started randomly shooting in a market full of innocent shoppers. We do not know how many exactly were killed or wounded, but the number was at least a few dozen.

DEPRESSING DARK DAYS FOR FAMILY

My brother's death and the Mau Mau attack had a huge impact on the whole family. Until then I was one of the top three students in my class. After the tragedies I lost interest in studies and withdrew from friends. Instead of looking forward to playing with other kids during break time I started dreading it. Standing alone at the edge of the playing field, unable to interact with others, I used to wait for break time to be over. In the classroom, I lost all interest and just waited for classes to end so I could go home. Going home, where everyone was drained of emotions, was also tough. My grades dropped and I was lucky to do better than one or two boys in the class. The whole family was in a similar condition, depressed and struggling to face the situation.

Two years later, my father paid a deposit from his savings and took a loan from the Railways to start construction of our new house in Pangani, Nairobi. The excitement of planning, building and finally moving into the dream house, provided a much-needed distraction. The family finally snapped out of depression. The new surroundings brought a new hope for the future. In the sixth class my grades started improving as I took on the challenge of making up for the lost years of education.

Jaihind and Kartar outside new dream house

Our family 1962
Sitting: Pinder, Pillo, Chachaji & Mama
Standing: Kinney, Chani, Jaihind, Pali, Kamal

CHAPTER 8

Journey Back To The Ancestral Land

By Jaihind

My first trip to India from Kenya was in December 1964 at the age of 18. My two brothers Chani and Pali and sister-in-law Jaswant accompanied me. I longed to travel on a ship similar to those I had always dreamed about after listening to my parents' stories of their journeys back and forth between Kenya and India. And just like our parents, we boarded our ship at Mombasa Harbor and left our belongings on the berth allocated to us in a large, hot open hall below deck.

Reliving our parents' journey, we selected a spot on a *falka* (loading bay covers) and spread out our sleeping mats. A few dozen passengers were already there. Soon, more people joined us and everyone started moving their mats to form similar aged groups, keeping males and females separated. The teenagers around us were mostly strangers from different towns of East Africa. It was not long before the cards and board games came out and total strangers soon became friends. Amongst the older folks, the formation of groups was based on their different mother tongues: Punjabi, Gujarati, and Konkani.

It was an eight-day long journey. Indian food was provided in the ship's galley. There was no cooking or cleaning to be done. The children were safe in community groups, so parents had time to enjoy the company of their peers, renewing old friendships, catching up on news and gossip from different towns.

Us teenagers followed a daily routine. Hot afternoons were spent looking for a shaded bench to read a book or to enjoy the tranquility of the sea, the peace broken only by the waves created by the momentum of the ship.

Occasionally, a school of flying fish would jump in and out of the water, as if their movements were choreographed for an audience. Seeing a huge fountain of water sprouting from a whale, passengers rushed over the railings for a better view, and as the ship sailed closer, we could see its large body.

After an early dinner, we enjoyed the cool evening breeze on the *falka* to resume our games and listen to stories told by grownups. A thin sheet covered my body, as my eyes absorbed the starlit sky. I admired the beauty of the universe, the soothing sounds of the sea. We would stay awake, late into the night, listening to stories narrated by other men: funny stories about their adventures, about the pioneering days, frequently exaggerating the details to outdo each other. And as they talked, slowly, one by one, we would all fall asleep.

Our sleep was always rudely interrupted by the hustle and bustle on the deck at dawn. I would lie in bed in the morning, waking up just in time to eat breakfast before the galley closed. After breakfast, a quick shower was followed by a leisurely walk around the ship.

On the eighth day, early in the morning our ship arrived at Bombay and from there we caught the evening train to Punjab, an express train which covered the 960-mile-long journey in 36 hours. During those 36 hours, I learned more about India than I ever could from books. It was an adventure, a unique experience, the joy of which will stay with me forever.

We bought triple tickets for each of us, for the journey. The standing ticket allowed us to board the train, the sitting ticket gave us an allocated seat, and the sleeping ticket entitled each of us to a clear berth at night, which we had to vacate in the morning. The train was overcrowded for most of the journey. Reserved seats vacated briefly for a washroom visit were quickly occupied by one or two standing passengers. We spent part of the journey two people to a seat. Similarly, sleeping berths were either not vacated at all or were vacated late. My brother Pali and I had to share a berth the first night. The following night, we acquired our berths very late and for only part of the night.

People boarded and departed from the train like performers on a stage, each new group introducing its own dress style, food and language to the train. To them we must have looked strange, with our Indian appearance but odd attire and mannerisms. With some of them, we just exchanged smiles and nods, while others struck up conversations by asking who we were, a question we had never faced in Kenya and did not have an easy answer to.

Who were we? Indian-Kenyans or Kenyan-Indians? Kenyan-Indians rolled off the tongue better, or maybe just off my tongue with my bias towards Kenya. The question of who we actually were got more complicated as we grew older and moved to other countries.

Fellow passengers would recommend what specialties to eat from vendors on the platform at each big city stop, and what landmarks to look out for from the train windows. Looking out of the window meant facing the soot from the coal fired steam engine pulling the train. Soot covered arms and faces could only be washed at taps on platforms, where the train made longer stops. The only option for changing clothes was in the toilets, something we did not bother with.

We arrived at our new family home in Chandigarh, and it was great to see the rest of the family after eight months. This was the longest separation from each other we had ever faced. Apart from time spent with the family, my best memories of my four months stay in India are from the time I spent in the villages.

In those days, there was very little mechanization on farms and most of the work was done by animals. As a teenager, it was fun to jump on and off carts pulled by bullocks, ride on the camels' backs, and play in the cool water pumped from the wells.

Our ancestral village home in Lalheri was spread over four locations. The main house was for cooking and sleeping. Like other houses, our living room, called the *baithak*, was in the village main street. There was a house for the animals and a separate small shed where animal dung was stored and molded into discs before drying for use as cooking fuel. The main house buildings had flat roofs and it was easy to jump from one roof to another. In hot summers, most people slept on the roof under the open skies. It reminded me of my time on the ship.

Due to the absence of toilets in the villages, people went to the fields to relieve themselves. It was a properly choreographed ritual: men and women carrying water in small metal vessels, going out in separate groups to different parts of the fields where they could find crops tall enough to give them some privacy. Squatting down to do their business, a small distance from each other but within hearing range, enabled them to carry on with discussions related to family, farming or local affairs. It was like listening to gossip and news of the day on a local radio. This unusual ritual was an enriching experience.

My only sad experience in India was witnessing the humiliating segregation of untouchable castes from the rest of the village. This brought back memories of life in Kenya. Having lived in a segregated society, we were familiar with the concept. Even then this new form of segregation seemed cruel.

My four months in India were over soon. With a repeat of the memorable train and ship journeys I was back home in Kenya, feeling confused for the first time in my life as to which country, out of the two, I belonged to.

CHAPTER 9

The Dawn Of Independence

By Jaihind

Up to the age of ten, Mau Mau activities played a big role in my life. For the next six years I was able to enjoy the wonderful life of Asian school kids in Kenya. We enjoyed the benefits of belonging to a close-knit group of diverse cultures and religions of India acting as one family to support, protect and provide for the needs of us youngsters. The fabulous sunny weather of Nairobi, daytime temperatures below 80° F degrees and nights above 60° F provided a big attraction to spend time outdoors. Time spent playing games using equipment and toys improvised from easily available material. Like good dreams my high school days in Kenya went by fast. Then around the age of sixteen came a big upheaval in the world around us. Kenya's independence from Britain on December 12, 1963 brought rapid changes to the country. Africans, previously treated as third class citizens quickly took control from their once powerful masters. African political prisoners and other capable individuals doing menial jobs with no prospects of advancement under British rule, suddenly moved into high level government jobs displacing Europeans and Asians. Without jobs, the displaced started moving to other countries. More about that later.

After WWII, like the Mau Mau movement in Kenya, the struggle for independence in European colonies in Africa intensified. In March 1957, Ghana was the first African country to be granted independence from Britain. This was rapidly followed by other countries on the continent.

AFRICANS MOVING TO POSITIONS OF RESPONSIBLITY

I was in high school when a group of us got together to form a music group. We entered a local competition in late 1962, where we met an African music group called 'The Shoe Shine Boys'. One evening after school, we visited them in their practice room.

There was a man sitting in a corner on a wooden crate enjoying the music. He was their sponsor and said he was interested in buying our guitar amplifier for his group. We negotiated a price, and he paid us a deposit, promising that we could collect the balance from him at his office. We left the amplifier with the group. He gave us his business card. It read: Muinga Chokwe, Speaker of the House of Parliament. We looked in awe at this powerful person in a high government position, sitting in a dingy room, wearing simple clothes, enjoying what he loved: music.

A few days later, straight after school, we arrived at the address on the card and found ourselves looking at a newly built, impressive looking multi-story government building. We showed the business card at the front desk and were directed to take the elevator to Mr. Chokwe's office. Inside we saw the gentleman, who just a few days ago had been seen perched on a rickety wooden crate, sitting behind a large oak desk with a panoramic view of the city from a window behind him. A brief greeting was followed by small talk. We were worried about wasting an important official's time, but he seemed to be in no hurry.

"Can we please receive the balance of the payment for the amplifier?" we asked.

"I am a poor man and do not have the money to pay you," he said with a hearty laugh and lifted his trouser legs to reveal that he was not wearing any socks, as he could not afford them. We were in our school uniforms. Our school blazer's elbows always used to get worn out and we often removed the side pockets, and sewed them as patches on the worn elbows. I pointed out the fake pockets on my blazer to reflect our poverty, and he laughed again.

"Alright, you've outdone me," he chuckled.

We spent a good half hour with him just chatting idly before he finally decided to part with his money.

In preparation for Kenya's independence, people like Chokwe, who had humble backgrounds, were suddenly placed in high ranking positions within the Kenyan government, positions they deserved, but had been denied during the colonial rule. I imagined they must have been uneasy in their new, unfamiliar roles and felt the desire to connect to their simple pre-independence lives.

Similarly, Africans suddenly promoted to higher positions of authority in police force would sometime overreact to situations to establish their status.

POLICE DESIRE TO ESTABLISH AUTHORITY LEADS TO ARREST

In August 1966, my friends Tejpal, Jagwant and I were on our way back from a wedding in Tanzania when we decided to stop over in Mombasa. The three of us were traveling on two motorcycles. We spent the first night in rooms provided by a local temple. The next morning, we headed towards the beautiful Bamburi beach, which in those days was isolated, tranquil and devoid of tourists.

Back then there were two small buildings on the beach about one mile apart. Each had showers, pit toilets, fresh water, and a cooking area. One was owned by the local municipality and the other by a local Hindu temple. We first stopped at the Hindu temple complex and then decided to ride across the sandy beach towards the other complex. Halfway there, we saw a large, newly erected building with a number of Africans swimming in the ocean and sunbathing on the beach, while others stood nearby formally dressed. We sped past them on our motorbikes toward our destination.

When we got there, we parked our bikes and had just gone in for a swim in the ocean when we heard sirens blaring and saw police cars approaching the beach. Who were they after? We wondered but carried on swimming without giving them another thought.

"Get out of the water!" They commanded as they pointed at us.

Once we were on the beach, the policemen, who were all Africans, surrounded us in a circle and started pushing and hitting us. This was followed by an alarming back seat ride in a police car towards Mombasa. Our two motor-bikes were loaded onto a truck, which followed us. The policeman in the front seat spoke to another officer on his walkie-talkie. "I have apprehended three Indian boys". The voice on the other side enquired about the charges. The next words casually uttered by the policeman in our car stunned and shook us.

"Attempted assassination of the President!"

On reaching the police station, we were asked to remove our belts and shoelaces and were locked up in a cell. Here we learned that the house on the beach belonged to President Kenyatta and the sunbathers were his family members being guarded by security personnel. After a short wait, we were taken to a room and were interrogated via a speaker phone by a man with a British accent. We did not see him, but he told us he was the Head of Kenya police in Nairobi. We explained to him in detail the events of the day, including the lack of any signage about trespassing and not being stopped or challenged by anyone on the beach.

"Things are changing in this country and you should be very cautious and sensitive to such situations," he said.

We then left the room and were told that there would be no charges and we could go home. It was understandable that Africans in new positions wanted to maintain law and order by establishing their authority. This at times led to overreaction on their part.

MASS EXODUS OF ASIANS AND EUROPEANS FROM KENYA

With independence came changes in rules around nationality. People with parents born in Kenya now qualified for Kenyan citizenship. Asians who had migrated from India when it was a British colony traveled on British passports. With a few exceptions, most Indians had parents born in India which meant they were British citizens and held on to their British passports. Our parents were born in India so we did not qualify for Kenyan citizenship.

Fear of retaliation due to the reversal of roles led many Europeans, especially those in civil service, to move back to Britain. A few went to other African countries like South Africa and Rhodesia (Zimbabwe) where the British rule seemed secure. Only a few stayed behind in Kenya. For Asians, the majority of whom were employed in middle level government jobs, the prospects looked bleak. The possibility of losing work under the "Africanization" program loomed on the horizon, and soon jobs occupied by Asian migrants would be reserved just for Kenyan citizens.

As a protest, Asians sent in mass resignations hoping to paralyze the government. The white bosses accepted resignations from Asians in low skilled and easy-to-fill jobs. This resulted in a large number of Asians being left without jobs, my father being one of them. Craftsmen, business owners and young professionals with better employment prospects moved to western countries like the United Kingdom, the United States and Canada to start afresh. Those who were older, with little prospect of starting a new profession, decided to move back to India and Pakistan. Asians sold their houses and businesses before leaving the country, creating a glut of property on the market, so prices fell sharply. Our house, which we had built six years earlier for Kenya Shillings 100,000 was sold for Kenya Shillings 60,000, which was hardly enough to pay back the loan taken out for its construction. From a peak of 180,000 Asians in Kenya in 1962 more than one hundred thousand had left the country by 1979. Our family was part of that exodus.

My parents left for India on May 6, 1964 with my two brothers Pillo and Kinney and sister Kamal. My older sister Pinder had got married in India the year before and was already settled there. My parents found a bride for my elder brother, Chani, who was married before they left for India. My younger brother Pali and I stayed behind with my brother Chani and his wife Jaswant to complete our high school studies. Pali left for Britain in 1966. I stayed in Kenya until 1968, to complete my high school and my Bachelors Degree in mechanical engineering from the University of East Africa (now the University of Nairobi). My elder brother and his wife who were both teachers, stayed in Kenya until 1979, before migrating to the US.

A large number of Indians migrated to Britain from their colonies in Africa. To curb immigration, in 1967, Britain introduced new rules for British passport holders to enter Britain. Only those with parents or grandparents born in Britain could enter Britain freely. The rest were subjected to restrictions after March 1968. My father, who was enjoying his retirement in India like a number of other Kenyan Indians, decided to go to the UK before the cut-off date to qualify for residency there. He had difficulty in adjusting to life in England and soon returned to India via Kenya.

FINAL DAYS OF MY PARENTS

Following the wedding of his grandson in Chandigarh, India on Christmas day 1996, my father became ill with what initially was thought to be the flu, but turned out to be meningitis. With most family members present for the wedding, on January 2, 1997, we all gathered around his bed. He told us how happy he was to have spent the last few weeks surrounded by the love of his family. The next evening, he went into a coma for ten days and passed away on January 13, 1997 at the age of 84.

My mother was diagnosed with Alzheimer's in June 2002 and died peacefully in Chandigarh, India at the age of what we believe to be 93, in her bed on July 13, 2009, exactly twelve and a half years after my father.

My elder brother Pillo, who was attacked by machetes, passed away in Birmingham, England on December 20, 2010 at the age of 69, from complications after a routine heart test.

LIFE AFTER KENYA

Our family's journey in Kenya ended in 1979, just over fifty years from when my father first set foot on Kenyan soil. The last members to leave Kenya were my elder brother Chani and his family.

Very few of the first generation of Indian immigrants to colonial Kenya are alive today. However their offspring, who I refer to as the "Kenyan

Generation", have now dispersed to every corner of the world. The willingness of their parents to uproot from India and successfully establish themselves in Kenya helped to encourage and prepare them for this mobility. The Kenyan Generation, a tribe of modern day nomads is now aging and retiring from successful careers and businesses all over the world. I wanted to capture this unique period of Kenyan history before it gets forgotten with the passage of time and hope that my narrative encourages the Kenyan Generation to enrich that nostalgic period of history by recording some of their own experiences. As for me, I left Kenya in 1968, at the age of twenty two. After ten years of postgraduate studies and employment in England, I moved to Germany. Five years later I was transferred to Detroit in USA, and then in 1994, to Charleston, South Carolina. I am now enjoying my retirement there with my wife Amerjeet and our family. While playing with my little granddaughter, I often wonder where her little feet will take her.

Siblings in England in 2010
Standing: Pali, Jaihind and Kinney
Sitting: Chani, Pillo, Kamal and Pinder

About The Author

Jaihind Sumal was born and brought up in Nairobi, Kenya. After completing a Bachelor's degree in Mechanical Engineering from University of East Africa (now University of Nairobi) he moved to London, England in 1968. He spent a year at University of London (King's College) to do his Master's Degree in Internal Combustion Engineering and soon began work in an engine research laboratory. While working at the laboratory he completed his Doctorate degree, again from University of London (King's College) in 1976. His work on development of a unique automotive fuel injector at another company in England, led to an offer of a position at Bosch in Germany in 1980, to work on the development of fuel injection system components. In 1985 Bosch transferred him to their development center in Detroit, followed by another transfer in 1994 to Charleston, South Carolina, where he lives now. He is enjoying his retired life with his family while pursuing his favourite hobby of working on cars and motorbikes, a hobby which started in his youth, in Kenya.

You can contact the author at: jsumalbk@gmail.com

Made in the USA
Middletown, DE
27 March 2019